Eating
DIAMONDS

LOREN CRUDEN

Illustrations by Leigh Cruden
Photographs by Gabriel Cruden

Whittles Publishing

Published by
Whittles Publishing Limited,
Roseleigh House,
Latheronwheel,
Caithness, KW5 6DW,
Scotland, UK
www.whittlespublishing.com

Design by
Melissa Alaverdy

Cover design & photography by
Melissa Alaverdy & Paul Akins

ISBN 1-904445-07-1

Printed by Bell & Bain Ltd., Glasgow

CONTENTS

CONTENTS

PREFACE

Neighbours! Who hasn't been tempted to report on their doings? But when was the last time you had a rattlesnake at your door, insisting on the right to enter; or a bear, perhaps, looking to borrow a cup of sugar? I suppose that's why I am in the fortunate position of being able to tell tales on my neighbours: in the safe knowledge that they are extremely unlikely to retaliate, as they are four-footed, winged or rooted beings that do not read books.

Although the natural world appears increasingly in contemporary writing, it is often draped like a scenic backdrop or stage setting for dramatic human exploits or, particularly in poetry, used as a metaphor or looking glass for human psychology. Much rarer are those gems of observation from quiet visitors to the wilds, which rejoice in nature being – well – natural.

What I hope to do with my own contribution is to ease into this spectrum the concept of nature as neighbourhood: an integrated neighbourhood, of which humans are a part. This is hardly a new perspective – it is as native to America as her indigenous peoples, and has travelled the plains and mountains of Europe with the wandering Celts.

I've lived in Scotland part-time since the mid-1990s and full-time, married to a Scot, since 2000. In America I was born and brought up on the east coast, and later lived in Michigan and the Pacific northwest. The human aspects of these neighbourhoods were very much part of what makes life good, and these stories are more than simply a record of one eccentric's experiences.

My outlook has been influenced by Indian medicine men and north Skye crofters, by close family in America and near strangers offering lifts down Highland single-tracks. As well, that outlook has been informed by living alongside bears, coyotes, rattlers, Hebridean otters – and sheep. An expansive neighbourhood, but an intimate conversation.

In the following pages I have tried to capture the essence of my neighbours, warts and beauty spots, the frustrations and joys of sharing a time and place with them, and most of all the tears and the laughter which bond every community. I hope you enjoy reading them as much as I enjoyed writing them.

So please, will you take a stroll with me around the neighbourhood?

Loren Cruden

ACKNOWLEDGEMENTS

Some of the poems in this collection have appeared in periodicals in the United States and Scotland: 'Gneiss', 'First Thought Mountain', 'She Waits', 'Winterkill', 'Spring Yet?', 'Standing In Place', 'The Silence of Light', 'Hebridean Economy', and 'Unfinished Sentences'.

Parts of 'Courage', 'Coming Home' and 'Singing to the Seals' appeared in my book, *Walking the Maze* (Destiny Books, Inner Traditions International; Vermont); part of 'November' appeared in my book *Compass of the Heart* (same publisher); and part of 'Shores', 'An American in Gaeldom', and 'Standing In Place' appeared in an article series in the *North Columbia Monthly* magazine.

Many thanks to Meg Bateman for her quote in 'An American in Gaeldom'; to my sister Leigh Cruden for her sensitive, superb illustrations; to my son Gabriel Cruden for his gorgeous photographic moments; to my husband Rob, without whom this manuscript never would've left my desk; and to Dr Keith Whittles, who kept it from returning there.

FOREWORD

There are as many ways to relate to nature as there are nature writers. And there are nature writers who relate to nature in more ways than one. Loren Cruden's relationship is multi-faceted, but it includes the essential one:

> *"I became used to — maybe addicted to — solitude after my son went off to university. Days, weeks, months going by when I saw almost no-one. I was disappearing into the landscape. An intimacy which, as in any relationship, evolved with duration, openness, humour; and humbleness in the face of something older and more powerful than yourself.*
>
> *Living with nature is participatory."*

Yes it is. And the way to participate fully is to spend time alone in nature's company. When you walk in wild places with human company, tribal loyalties hold sway. The wildness is inevitably discussed, and the discussion diminishes your ability to understand that which is seen but unspoken. Alone with nature there are no barriers, perceptions sharpen, understanding deepens, and nature begins to matter for its own sake.

I sail with William Hazlitt in all this. In his essay of around 1820, *On Going A Journey*, he wrote:

> *"Instead of an awkward silence, broken by attempts at wit or dull common-places, mine is that undisturbed silence of the heart which alone is perfect eloquence…"*

Then:

> *"…Is not this wild rose sweet without a comment? Yet if I were to explain to you the circumstance that has so endeared it to me, you would only smile. Had I not better then keep it to myself, and let it serve me to brood over, from here to yon craggy point, and from thence onward to the far-distant horizon? I should be but bad company all that way, and therefore prefer being alone."*

And then:

> *"…'Let me have a companion of my way,' says Sterne, 'were it but to remark how the shadows lengthen as the sun goes down.' It is beautifully said: but in my opinion, this continual comparing of notes interferes with the voluntary impression of things upon the mind and hurts the sentiment."*

It is the task of the nature writer to take the ideas engendered by "the voluntary impression of things upon the mind" received in "that undisturbed silence of the heart" back to the writing desk, to re-order and re-colour them and write them down in ways which will give readers pause for thought, cause for consideration.

Here is Loren Cruden writing about a Skye gale:

> *"...All day unyielding. It is extraordinary when air takes command: like the impact of falling into water from a great height – something you expect to give way suddenly clobbers you like a concrete block..."*

Yes, you think. I know that Skye wind. And when she sketches an image of "croft houses like a dot-to-dot picture connected by racing collies", yes, you think, I know those houses.

And because she is an American who has come to live on Skye she can startle Scottish sensibilities with a specifically transatlantic image:

> *"Winter mountain night, its breath rimes the firs. Bears are dreaming in the mountain's pockets..."*

Or this:

> *"...In the middle of the night, coyote mother comes to our tent and tries to drag away the heavy water jug. I hear the sound of it and stick my head out of the tent, coming face to face with her. She freezes, still gripping the jug.*
>
> *" 'No, Coyote,' I whisper to her. 'We need our water.' She drops it and evaporates into the cold night. Next morning I finger her tooth marks on the plastic handle."*

There is a certain gentle charm at work in these pages. The participatory relationship with nature is compassionate rather than confrontational. Would you have *whispered* to the coyote?

Eating Diamonds is a thoughtful, quietist book, characterised by a four-line poem:

THE ONLY DESTINATION

For ten years
walking this mountain,
my only destination
has been peace.

Its simplicity says more than it appears to say. Sip it slowly, the way you might sip glacial melt water from your hand.

Jim Crumley
Balquhidder, 2004

DEDICATION

For Barbara,
and the bobcat.

Standing in Place

Swan-feather day
with its wind,
bog-cotton,
orchids our boots brush
in going,
in coming back.
Stones in my pockets,
the ground of days loved.

INTRODUCTION

When my son was a young child we lived in northern lower Michigan. First on 80 acres of woodland and fields, later on 20 acres where salmon would surge and slither up a shallow creek under the cedars to spawn and die.

Winter in northern Michigan is a substantial matter. Driving a 4x4 high-clearance Scout with its macho studded snow tyres home from a stock-up to the shop one day, I bottomed out on the road's deep-packed snow and had to walk. I stuffed as many groceries as I could into my coat pockets – even up my sleeves – hoisted my wee son Gabriel onto my hip, and set off.

Hard going, the snow thigh-deep. I floundered and paused, floundered and paused. It was cold, and in such temperatures you do not want to sweat and do not want to be still too long – unless you have a death wish.

Our cabin was on a hill on the fringe of the forest. Hand built of salvaged planks, cedar trunks, scrounged window glass. Eventually it came into view, but I was struggling. Panting. Floundering shorter and shorter distances between pauses. I shifted Gabriel from hip to hip; my arms felt muscle-less, though bulked by the oranges in my sleeves. I was fading.

At the base of the hill there was a long pause, exhaustion locking me in place, cold seeping like ice-water through my clothes, to the bone. I was finished, couldn't move. In snow so weighty and deep there was no sitting down. It was almost to my waist – I simply leaned, gripping Gabriel to my chest, looking up at the cabin beside the bare trees. Thinking: how beautiful, the land in its winter purity of line; and how strange that you could die gazing at your house so close, unattainable because of zillions of tiny white sparkles.

"Where's Lori's legs?" piped Gabriel from the bundled depths of his snowsuit. "Legs all gone!" he cheerily noted, peering down, fascinated at a truncated mother.

Kids. Always gate-crashing your most poignant moments of futility.

There were plenty of those moments in our way of life. Where at times the wilds gave us strength and solace in the face of human misery; at times human friends, family and neighbours gave support in the face of elemental peril; and in general the integration of humanity and "wilderness" wove a richness and wholeness of experience. Love, within that integration, needs to be fiercely and demonstrably unconditional. Principles were plumbed on a daily basis. You knew where you stood in nature, and beauty was a life-force in itself. You discovered capacities and stretched them; learning how to proceed harmoniously in a natural reality where humans are an often clumsy minority participant. This was the context of my life for 25 years.

In the year 2000 I married a Scotsman. A rock climber. Though I had lived on a grey stony mountain in north-eastern Washington state for 10 years, I'd never tried rock climbing in equipped sporting terms. Three factors are favoured by mountain dwellers like myself when considering necessarily vertical movement: what's the fastest route, the easiest route, and the safest route. I'd stand at the base of a Scottish cliff with my husband, who was patiently trying to answer my questions about his vertical art, and we'd peruse the cliff together. "How about going up that grassy bit and around those boulders at the side?" I'd suggest. Obviously the fastest, easiest and safest route to the top.

My husband would look pained.

It suddenly dawned on me that the idea was to find the hardest, most challenging and most athletically aesthetic route up. I was sincerely gobsmacked. This was the moment when I began to ponder differences between living with nature and seeking it for specialised purposes – whether recreational, academic, spiritual, commercial or therapeutic.

I have to say that, while I never got the hang of rock climbing, my husband – when visiting our mountain in Washington – found himself well suited to our way of life there. Perhaps the jump away from electricity, phones, computers, TVs, traffic, consumerism, is not so great and unthinkable as imagined.

I didn't embark on a "primitive" way of life out of idealism or romantic notion. It happened because I was poor. It is far better being poor in the countryside than in a town or city. You can fashion a shelter (I've lived in tents, a bus, a barn, a tipi and various home-made cabins), grow food, keep beasts, harvest fuel, haul water and be inspired and entertained by your habitat. By the time we moved to the mountain in Washington I was still poor, but wouldn't have brought in electricity or phone lines even if I could've afforded them.

During those decades in the States I worked, in overlapping succession, as a homebirth midwife, a herbalist, a spiritual teacher and a writer. I became used to – maybe addicted to – solitude after my son went off to university. Days, weeks, months going by when I saw almost no one. I was disappearing into the landscape. An intimacy which, as in any relationship, evolved with duration, openness, humour; and humbleness in the face of something older and more powerful than yourself.

Living with Nature is participatory.

To compartmentalise life as we have done in the modern world has taken some thousands of years of effort, but it doesn't follow that this was effort well spent. Having humans and the rest of nature in separate boxes; having work and recreation, home habitat and natural habitat in different compartments, has denied – even endangered – the integrity of life.

What I set out to do with this collection was to walk lightly, and from many angles, through some reflections on living close to the earth. The pieces relate incidents contributing to my sense of place in natural community. Family played a part, as did travel – the earth's habitats so various and interwoven, each with a perspective and power to shape human values and culture. The essays about Scotland look at the inseparability of landscape and culture in how we see ourselves and envision our future.

Other stories are about encounters with wildlife, the way indoors and outdoors can merge to create a larger realm of sympathetic relationship with life. With "being among", and belonging.

PART ONE   PEOPLE

SURVIVING

Easily splintered as light, I am
trying to hold wildflower hues,
streamwater textures.
Mosquitoes feel my heat but
I'm floating
nearly invisible,
sun between my bones –
that thin.
The cat leaps to my shoulder –
weight and vibration – urgency;
does he have a name for me?
Border of spring, birdsong
fringing the trees, light
balanced on tulip rims,
swallows marrying cool morning to
broad noon, stitches the
spread of summer will pull loose.
I have waited for this day and
am tongue-tied with how to greet it.
Sometimes survival seems
easier than
all this gentle possibility.

EATING DIAMONDS

I come from a land-rich family. Not in terms of baronial estate – we've always been money-poor – but in landscape wealth. Gathering habitat details the way a banker stacks coins, and at the end of the day sitting amid a trove.

My mother is a great one for collecting names of things: trees, birds, wild flowers, star constellations, bugs. And if she doesn't think the thing well-named, she'll sometimes go ahead and change it. Like calling juniper trees "alteras", which she thought more dignified. Her mother taught herself the names of all the ferns. My sister has a fat bank account of names too – she upped the ante by additionally learning about animal tracks, mushroom identification and the sinister lives of lichens. Mom retaliated by becoming expert on bullfrogs.

Growing up, I didn't learn how to earn money (or be a housewife) but did rake in scenic details. My early landscapes were Floridian: beaches, ocean, soupy lakes, swamps, scrublands of sandspur, palmetto, rattlesnakes, citrus groves, cottonmouths, chiggers, jays, mockingbirds, mosquitoes, a teeming inventory, much of it prickly, surly or downright poisonous. We kids went into the landscape nearly naked and quickly smartened up about where to put bare feet.

We moved north when I was ten, over my first mountains to my first snow and a wealth of cold creeks and deciduous trees. A generous landscape, but stern weather, strict seasons. We four kids flew the nest: my sister went into wildlife research and rehab but her ethics prevented her from accepting most of the work on offer. She took care of birds of prey, led wildlife tours on the Dechutes River, and exerted herself in spotted owl and cavity-nester research for the Forest Service, until turning to wildlife illustrating and domestic animal care. Her owner-built house in the Oregon high desert is an oasis for deer, birds, golden mantles, coyotes and whatever else comes by for a drink, a browse, a compassionate reception.

My brothers ended up with more urban fates, but my younger brother became bewitched by scuba diving, undersea dreamscapes with their unearthly flickering colours. He watches fish instead of birds. My older brother visited Africa several times to admire the landscapes and wildlife there. He sent photos of elephants in a lake and tells us what we're supposed to do if meeting a rhino. He's also been to the Galapagos Islands, encountering bluefooted boobies and giant tortoises, exotic currency. When he and I were talking on the phone one day, he told me about a bird in his yard (typical of the family to discuss birds instead of neighbours). "What kind of bird?" I asked (of course).

"Brown," he said.

The naming thing mainly took with us daughters. But the noticing, the close interest and, particularly, the delight, is shared in common.

My father is big on birds too. He feeds them, makes notes about them in his journal. Keeps track of them. But his special connection is with trees and he used to make his livelihood from flowers. Chrysanthemums. My earliest memories are of rows of golden 'mums brilliant in the velvet southern night, blooming under the lights he'd strung over the field. He had moved to Florida to try out his idea of getting 'mums to bloom out of season by manipulating their day length. He couldn't afford to build a greenhouse up north, so came south to grow the flowers outdoors. My father's idea worked – he pioneered this commercial technique – but never reaped much income from it. Just the gold memory of those flowers blooming in their midnight velvet jewel case. Nature's seasonal vagaries defeated him financially – farming is a precarious business when you don't have much capital. My father has the touch when it comes to plants, but there's no cajoling the elements. Later in life, when my father's house in Oregon burned down due to a forest fire, the biggest heartbreak for him was losing the trees.

He used to take us fishing when we were kids. Three generations of his family had camped and fished at Tupper Lake, in northern New York State. Our generation fished from an open aluminium boat, my father rowing, surreptitiously manoeuvring along the shore, whispering to us about where to cast our lines, tying extraordinary lures onto our hooks with which to beguile the quarry.

I always threw back what I caught. It was the act of fishing I liked. The setting off at dawn across the misty lake; the mystery of the fish, unseen beneath the wavering shadows of boulders and larches. My father's patience and ease on the water; the lulling motion of the boat and the heart-stopping lashing strike of a fish. I liked the casting and reeling in, the way the lures wriggled, vibrated and sometimes violently propellered through the tea-coloured water. Magic. Except when my cast was successful and I was confronted with a hooked fish's pain. It was up to us whether to keep and cook the fish or release it.

One night my father took me out in the tippy, fragile canoe to view the full moon. I'd been out on the lake at night only once before, to spy on the beavers. This time it was just my father and me. The moon seemed exceptional in brightness and largeness, spilling coins on the rippling dark lake. I clutched the camera while my father paddled, then steadied the boat while he clicked photographs. Flawlessly alive on a shivering path of silver.

It gave me a taste for booty. One day, as a grown-up, I went for a walk on the mountain where my son and I lived. A storm had conjured a new world during the night. Sunlight on snow: a glittering carpet. Trees shed their snow loads in sudden shrugs, branches springing free, showering more jewels through the twinkling air. Heaven's vaults had emptied onto the land.

I brushed off a rock, put my wool hat beneath me and sat admiring these riches. I had a craving to taste them. I scooped a handful of snow into my mitten and licked it. Worries about taxes and car insurance vanished: I was sitting on a mountainside eating diamonds.

MY MOTHER'S POND

Paddling the small circle
of the lake
I see six turtles
on their logs
and bees on the waterlilies.
I pass like a June afternoon,
wake less resolute
than the muskrat's.
Today tastes just like
honey made from waterlilies.

COURAGE

Three things my mother wouldn't abide were cruelty, lies and fear. She wasn't big on us reading Sunday funnies before church either. But the thing about fear had a more lasting impact. I remember as a child in Florida sitting at the table near an open screened window having to "calmly" eat my lunch while a rattlesnake lounged on the sill outside. And the time my sister and I were hiking with our mom, and my sister, walking just in front of me, stepped on a rattler. Leigh levitated an astonishing height and shot horizontally an astonishing distance before returning to earth. Our fear evident, my mother sat us down (some ways away from the snake) and reminded us about Daniel in the lion's den, which to her mind had exemplary bearing on our situation.

My mother had an admirable calm and fortitude in daunting circumstances. When she was prevented by wind from rowing back to shore during an excursion with me on a shallow and exceedingly murky Florida lake, she slid overboard and hauled the boat across the lake by its painter, which I'd have died rather than do. The lake bottom was deep ooze, the water thick with leeches, slimy weeds and water moccasins: she slogged thigh to waist-deep in it. I sat in the boat, trailing my toy boat on a string, and thought my mom the bravest person I'd ever met. Maybe she is. Her courage has always made me feel wimpy and inspired, challenged and protected.

She took in injured wildlife with no prejudice. Cuteness or gratitude were not prerequisite. I learned that, regardless of species (even human), you do what you think is needed because that's what's right to do, not because you'll get any warm fuzzies from it. She never tried to tame or keep anything. I remember numerous birds, a fox, a snapping turtle and various rodents passing through her care.

I think the only time I felt betrayed by my mother was when a black-billed cuckoo died and she told me it had recovered and flown away. The cuckoo had crashed into the passenger side of our car, toppling through the window into my young lap. It was mortally injured but we brought the bird home and I was closely involved with nursing it. I had a tremendous personal need for it to live. But it didn't, and my no-nonsense mother, who never lied, lied to me. I found the dead cuckoo wrapped in newspaper in the bin.

For a time after my son was born, my mother and I were neighbours on eighty acres of rural land in northern Michigan. She and my father were divorced and she lived in a cabin she herself designed and helped build. Late one night she heard terrible screaming in the forest and went out into the woods alone to see what the trouble was. Mating porcupines, she told me the next day.

Porcupines were a trial. They chewed anything hinting of salt: wooden barrow handles, wooden tool handles, wooden boat hulls, oars, porches, door frames and, once during winter, both brake linings on my car. My mother heard rustling in her garden beside the cabin one dark night. Thinking it was those pesky porcupines again, she leaned out her window and commandingly chastised them.

It was a bear.

Oh well. Even bears are subject to my mother's chastisements. It hustled back into the woods; my mother felt bad about scaring it.

I was the one awakened another night – by something scratching at my back door. Half asleep, thinking it was the cat, I padded barefoot through the kitchen and opened the door. A porcupine obligingly trundled in. Dazed by this incongruity, my mind couldn't seem to proceed past this point. The porcupine seemed befuddled also, as if suddenly realising its predicament, but I couldn't persuade it to go back out the door. The porcupine lumbered to a corner of the kitchen and stood like a recalcitrant child presenting its back to me, a formidable, bristling display poignantly undermined by the spreading yellow puddle around its paws; the porcupine was so scared it was piddling.

We were at an impasse. I phoned my mother, sure she would know what to do. Ten minutes later, my front door swung open. "I am dressed for porcupine!" Barbara announced with a grand flourish of the broom she carried. She had donned protective raincoat and rubber boots over her pyjamas. She herded the porcupine out the door, gently whacking it with her broom.

I had a horse for a while. Half thoroughbred and half quarter-horse, but the high-strung thoroughbred in her dominated. She'd been abused as a foal and this added to her stratospheric tendencies. She was still young when I got her; I hoped to train her to be a saddle horse. While fencing a pasture I kept her in a barn stall next to the goats, and tried to picket her outdoors to graze during stall cleanings.

To say this horse was jumpy is to say Jack the Ripper was whimsical. She got slightly tangled in her picket rope one day, freaked, and became extraordinarily tangled. Hearing the commotion, I ran out of the barn; my mother hurried over from her cabin. The horse was crazed, rope now wound

around a couple of her legs, tight around her windpipe, choking her. She was down, heaving, hooves maniacally thrashing, eyes rolling. I was petrified.

My mother darted in and freed her.

I don't recall how – whether by cutting the rope or the halter, or what. I just know I hesitated and she did it. I felt wee again, my mother the bravest person I knew. This time she spared me Daniel in the lion's den.

In May

In May
the wild rose blooms and
geese surge
scattering petals of light.
In May
green dreams wake
soft as babes who
grow in their sleep.
And I see you
bending like a mother
over the trusting face of
a flower
in May when the
wild rose blooms.

GRACIOUS MOMENTS

My son Gabriel is a photographer. He got serious about it as a teenager, taking pictures of wildlife. Taking pictures may be too aggressive a description; perhaps it is more a matter of receiving pictures – participating in acts of light. Driving along, Gabriel will see clouds, or rock lichen, something like that; he'll stop the car and get out to receive a picture.

What he receives is light being clouds, or light being lichen, in a way that makes the momentariness of grace seem both rare and pervasive. This is accomplished by stillness; not just the camera's, but the attention's.

Often, stillness in teenage boys is stuporous, occurring in early morning or in conjunction with substance abuse. The photographer's stillness in teenage Gabriel was different. I think Gabriel sees nature as though it is his, but in the sense of relatedness, not possession; in affectionate detail.

Gabriel notices a flower amid a mountainside of flowers. He sets up his tripod and camera and begins to participate in a graceful moment. He has great patience in this. Through his camera he frames the subject, foreground, background, the compositional elements. He chooses shutter speed, depth of field, focal point, use or not of flash, zoom – all that stuff. A breeze comes up the mountainside; he waits. The sun ducks behind a cloud; he waits. During this, he is becoming more and more still – very zen. Then – click, which in another language might sound like "amen" or "namaste" or "mitakwe oyasin".

When people look at pictures received like that, the stillness is shared, an intimacy wherein, because of stillness, no boundaries are violated.

Babies engage with just about anything. Objects haven't been catalogued and, on the whole, taken for granted or dismissed. There is an innocence in photographs also. Tree bark, doorway shadows, ice edging a puddle, commonplace aspects of the visual day are investigated and cherished along with uncommon treasures.

People responding enthusiastically to wildlife pictures are often cheered by photographic evidence that nature's vitality continues to accompany us on the earth. To think that nature is out there is to maintain the option of relationship with it. One can ponder the option along with the photograph, and wonder what it must've been like for the photographer standing so close to something scary, or magnificent, or secretive, or strange. In the plethora of wildlife images is the impression of a great supply of wilderness; an illusion; indeed, a dangerous deception – but it keeps us thinking about nature. Even if so much of what commercial photographers do is contrived, a distorted reality, an exploitation, images of the wild continue to arouse us, sometimes making us think again, connect.

When Gabriel was thirteen I travelled with him and my mother to England and Scotland. We visited Stonehenge, an ancient sacred site where prodigious stone slabs were planted upright by Neolithic folk thousands of years ago. While Gabriel received photographic moments (with his first camera) my mother and I gazed at the huge stones. After a long silence my mother remarked, "This certainly makes modern religion look flabby."

Vision's perspective can stand contrasts from time to time. Much can be realised during the receptive stillness it takes to fully focus. I don't always know what it is Gabriel is focusing on when he stands in a frosty field or on the margins of a swamp with his camera, but the images combine in the alchemy of his experience to produce an inner vision of what life is and what can be understood from that. His partnership with a camera asserts that what is seen is – in its integrity, as is – valuable.

There was a grouse on our land who used to ambush us at a particular section of the driveway. She would strut from the underbrush and pose in front of the car. In her diminutively majestic way she would pause, projecting the idea of photo opportunity. Sometimes Gabriel would get out with his camera to receive her moment. Perhaps she had dreams of becoming a famous grouse, a Christy Brinkley of birds. Or maybe she was just trying to distract us from her nest.

Gabriel used to teach photography. When he talked about light his animation was fervent; his hands framed his thought. No day is long enough for all the natural moments of dignity and grace he sees in it, yet he is frugal with his use of photography. The seeing is its own art.

THE ONLY DESTINATION

For ten years
walking this mountain,
my only destination
has been peace.

Chop Wood, Carry Water, Climb Everest

The Sherpas called Dave Gordon "Ballou" – bear – because of his playful, strong, ready embrace. Dave was fifty-five when he went to Everest, but looked ten years younger, with a physicality that, bear-like, had nothing to prove.

Dave and his wife Emily live on a mountain – small in his scale of experience – in a home-made cabin. When he lies in bed in the morning, looking up at the pole rafters, Dave feels the personality of his home. He'd like to build another cabin, sensing that with all the difficulty and pain he's gone through since the first project, the second cabin will have even stronger character. His mountaineering mind believes this, but alongside the Old World "struggles are to be overcome" mentality is a belief in receptivity and stillness.

"One day I led a group of teenagers up Mount Adams," Dave told me. "I insisted that we stay on the mountain the night after getting off the summit. It would've been easy to get back to the cars and get out of there, and the teenagers were pretty upset with me for making them stay.

"Next morning I woke early, right about sunrise, and crawled out of the tent. I walked a ways and sat on a rock. Big mountains throw a tremendous shadow at sunrise. I was watching the shadow spread out on the flats below me when I suddenly had this experience of being part of the mountain, a strong sense of inseparability, like the mountain and myself were part of the same entity. It went on for a number of minutes, quite intense."

"I was hoping that feeling would happen with Chomolungma (Everest) but it mostly didn't. There was a time or two. When I was on the face leading to the North Col, which is at about 23,000 feet, I felt the mountain exert some of its muscle. But my expectations didn't work out: it wasn't anything like the Mount Adams experience and I was disappointed."

Dave talked about the warping of subjective time that happens during expeditions, how days seem like weeks, the stretching of experience over a framework of effort. When effort becomes extreme and the breath strains for sustenance in the miserly resources of high altitude, communion becomes elusive.

"When I left on the expedition to Everest I hoped that the lack of oxygen would shut down the logical side of the brain so that other things could happen that are quieter, underneath what J. C. Pierce calls 'roofbrain chatter'. My conception is that you meditate to get rid of roofbrain chatter in order to get on to the business of satori. I was hoping that getting rid of the oxygen would do the same thing, but it didn't seem to happen.

"Even at Base Camp everything was so much of an effort that I found it hard to make an extra effort to get away from Base Camp, away from people and just sit and meditate. I tried to do some of it when I was moving between camps. It was 12–14 miles between Base Camp and Advance Base Camp (ABC), and 12,000 feet of elevation gain. But I was so whacked-out (maybe I'm just not an advanced enough student of this stuff) that maybe I didn't meditate enough for it to work out. You try to get up enough energy to do the things you have to do in order to go anywhere."

Dave is a teacher at an alternative school in the non-alternative community of Colville, Washington. The kids he teaches are drop-outs, teens too alienated or angry or non-conforming or non-compliant for mainstream education. Many of the girls are pregnant or have children. The school is housed in an extraordinarily cramped office building, yet, until recently, provided on-site day-care.

The school's hallway proudly displays photographs of some of Dave's students rapelling down a rock face outside town. Dave carried the school flag with his climbing gear when, in 1995, he participated in the Mount Everest expedition commemorating George Mallory, who disappeared on Everest in 1924. Mallory's grandson was one of the climbers on the expedition with Dave. I asked Dave if death was much on his mind during the Everest climb.

"I think I came to terms with death a long time ago. I can't count on my fingers and toes the number of acquaintances – and a few friends – who have died on mountains. Part of the reason I went back to the Himal was because of the Manaslu expedition in 1990 when we lost two members and a Sherpa in an avalanche. I had to drag their bodies off the mountain.

"We had a Buddhist cremation ceremony at the base of the mountain with seven lamas who came considerable distances on foot for that ceremony. This spring, when we were having a puja, a Buddhist blessing ceremony, at the base of Everest, I began to cry because it reminded me of that Manaslu experience.

"I don't think it was just a matter of coming to terms with my own mortality. During the puja I experienced a strong feeling that big mountains, like the yin-yang symbols, are places where life and death meet. I don't know if this is right, wrong or indifferent. It's just the way I felt. The connection between the living and dead – I almost physically felt them instead of just thought about them.

"I don't think you can climb very long unless you come to hard terms with death on the mountain, because if you're not aware that it can happen you're an idiot.

"When I started climbing, in 1961, American climbing was heavily influenced by European climbing, especially the European guide ethic, which is unselfish to the point of, I suppose, idiocy by American cultural standards. The guide was expected to – and sometimes did – lay down his life for the client. That's really harsh, but that's where I started, and the instant gratification thing seems to be at the opposite pole.

"Last year at mountain school there was a young lady who was extremely frustrated – in spite of incredibly nasty weather and obvious avalanche danger – when we didn't continue the graduation climb on Mount Athabasca. I saw her again, during the Everest Expedition's shakedown climb on Rainier. She was bouncing around up there, climbing Rainier. On Monday she was flying out to Bolivia to climb a 21,000 foot mountain. I looked at her and didn't say anything but I thought, 'Wow, what's the rush? Why not have paid your dues?'

"Part of paying your dues is to assume that, because of lack of oxygen up high, only experience is going to get you through the tight spots. If you don't have any experience to fall back on, what are you doing?

"In one of Carlos Castaneda's books, Don Juan Matuus says that your death is your ally. One of the things he claimed was that he could see his death stalking him over his left shoulder. He could see the flicker. He said, therefore, 'When I can see death stalking me, I don't have time to waste on bullshit. I have to live my life correctly.'

"Our expedition leader on Everest was deeply concerned about safety on the mountain. Early in the expedition he said, 'If the devil popped out of the ground and made me a deal that we'd get four people to the summit, get them down with everybody safe and missing no fingers and toes, I'd sign away my soul on the dotted line.' He was gut-wrenchingly worried about losing people.

"I felt for him. I didn't want to lose anybody, either, after Manaslu. One of my least favourite activities is dragging my friends' bodies off mountains. It impacts me in ways I don't understand, far more than just forcing me to realise mortality.

"So our leader felt that only the strongest should be on summit teams. Some of the other guys said, 'Screw you, bud, we're going anyway.' So, everybody but Jon Rosen and I were put on the first two summit teams. We were on the third, but Jon got sick and the Sherpas were all spent. We started with ten high altitude Sherpas and had five left who were able to climb by summit day, so there was nobody for me to climb with.

"If I'd been pushy about it I probably could've said 'Hey, I'm going on the summit teams too.' But I feel that life is run by what looks like circumstances at the time, but are really the Tao, or whatever you want to call that kind of thing.

"One of the hard things on this trip was all the publicity we had to go through in order to pay for the expedition. I really disliked it because it seemed like a real ego trip to tell people you're going on this thing. Yet, there were a lot of people in the community who were supportive – not because they thought I was a great guy or anything, but because I was pursuing the dream, and they felt you ought to pursue dreams even though all of us get stuck in this rut so much we can't see blue sky.

"During the puja ceremony I was feeling a connection with everyone here, from that windswept barren place in Tibet. But the question is, what are you doing it for? Why spend all that money and time in a God-awful hostile environment? What are the strokes? Just to say you've stood on the summit of the world? My excuse for going was that maybe I'd learn something. Now I feel kind of dumb because I'm back and I don't know what the lessons were.

"Another reason I went was because it was Tibet, a deeply Buddhist place that has been incredibly violated. We learned things about what the Chinese have been doing over there that you don't hear in the media. I was one of the 'haves' of course. The yak herders do everything possible to steal from you. At the same time, we were told through the Tibetan Outreach Centre, that when exiled Tibetans were asked if we should be going over there, putting money into the Chinese coffers, the Tibetans said 'absolutely yes'. That what we would learn and bring back to western countries was far more valuable than that pittance. It felt good to hear that, but I didn't hear it until we were already there, the decision made and the money paid. It did salve my conscience some.

"Here at the school they heard a story that wasn't true, that I didn't summit because I was helping a guy with deep thrombophlebitis. That's one of the many illnesses that can kill you at high altitude. Yeah, I was there with Dr Jon Rosen, who was looking after the guy. We didn't do much for him – couldn't, he was too stubborn. He refused to go down from 20,000 feet when he should've, so was clearly at risk for some weeks. The perception here was that 'our Dave' was there helping someone else. That's not what happened, but I did wind up being a nurturing kind of guy because I was supporting the summit teams, giving up my own wishes and goals.

"I argued with myself, with my body, in a conversation I had at ABC about going home. 'The hell with this – I'm tired of being cold and out of breath and struggling all the time. This is idiotic – what are we doing here?' And then coming to the realisation that it was just lack of self confidence because we were going up next day to a place I hadn't been able to get to in two tries before, with heavy packs. Next day, we weren't able to go up because of the weather, but I got pretty high and realised I could do it after all. There was a kind of relaxation and it was a lot easier after that. I had known I wasn't really going to quit, but I sure was trying hard to: it seemed stupid to be there.

"Climber philosophy says that if you don't enjoy the act of climbing you ought to quit, because climbing is not about bagging summits. The summit is just the place where you turn around and go down. There were days on Everest when

I thoroughly enjoyed what I was doing, when I felt connected to the mountain, felt very happy with just the act of climbing.

"Certainly, the third cycle up, I was in better spirits than ever, especially after a rough day at Base Camp. I left ABC with Jon Rosen ahead of me a bit. I found him on a rock up the first rise, twenty minutes from camp, and he was really sick. He went down to Base and I continued up the North Col. I realised, just as I was putting on crampons and harness, getting ready for the face of the North Col, that I didn't have anybody to climb with! I was out of luck – had to forget it.

"You know, it's funny, because there was relief in the realisation that I probably wasn't going to get a shot at the summit, AND a feeling of disappointment. Relief and disappointment at the same time. I wasn't going to have to go through that God-awful horrible summit day, but I was disappointed that I wasn't. There wasn't a very good chance of dying, now, but I also would maybe miss some experience, some part of the mountain's character and personality.

"The cliché from us old guys on the mountain is that there are old climbers and there are bold climbers, but no old, bold climbers. But it's questionable whether I get more out of climbing when I take fewer risks. It's kind of funny because, as a guy who's climbed for thirty-four years, obviously I'm a resource. 'Well, hey Dave, what do you think about this or that? Exercise your judgement, oh wise one'. It's never black and white. Exactly what the mountain's up to requires not only experience, but sensitivity.

"I've felt mountains being extremely hostile at times. I made a first ascent on Rainier in 1978, and there was a point when I felt the mountain was out to get us. I don't know why it was being malevolent but there was a period there – you always wonder: WAS the mountain really being malevolent? The place we were in felt very bad, inhabited by evil spirits, as it were. I just wanted to get the heck out of there.

"The only way was up. Sometimes you're forced to do things, at which point you have to use your adrenaline to help you get through places you otherwise couldn't. Instead of letting it lock you in a spread-eagle position, you use the experience you have to get yourself out of the jam and let the adrenaline drive it.

"George Mallory, the grandson of the original Mallory, was totally focused on the Everest summit. He was going to the summit and that's all there was to it. He made remarkable time from the high camp at 26,000 feet to the summit: he went in four and a half hours. He just blasted up there, dragging one of the Sherpas along. Superman of the mountains. If there is a difference between that kind of focus, and obsession, I don't know what it is.

"The Sherpas are paid pretty big money, for Nepal. But most of the people who die on expeditions are Sherpas. We championed safety measures on this expedition. Still, we only had five out of ten Sherpas in shape to climb when summit day arrived. They had worked so hard and were so burned out. That says a lot. Who puts in all the camps? The Sherpas do. We walk to the top on the back of Sherpas, literally. As Buddhists they are committed to helping others. They're far more helpful than they need to be for the money they're getting paid.

"There was an incident – I can't remember what year it was – with a Sherpa who died on the south side of the mountain. Rather than carry the body down, some Caucasians – I think they were European – kicked the body off the mountain and it rolled down into the Western Cwm. The Sherpas were very upset. Working with Westerners, I've seen that they tend to look down on the Sherpas, think the Sherpas are inferior and you can kick their bodies off mountains. Deeper than that, there's an inability to recognise connection.

"That upsets me. The Sherpa who died on Manaslu possibly – not probably, but possibly – wouldn't have died if he'd had on a transceiver. They're bloody expensive, but we might've been able to get him out quicker if he'd been wearing one. I've since decided that if I'm on a mountain where there's avalanche danger, we're going to supply transceivers for the Sherpas or I'm not going.

"That's one of the things with the commercial expeditions: you pay your money, get fit, grab your personal gear, and go. You don't work with anyone, except to call your glorious leader once in a while to ask when you're leaving, and that's it. We had one guy who summited on a commercial expedition, then came out with us. Why stick around?

"We had one member we should've booted off the expedition, who eventually jumped ship and joined a commercial expedition. He was 29 going on 14, emotionally. The feeling among the climbers was, 'I can't trust this guy – I won't rope up with him', so he couldn't find anyone to climb with. He was supposed to help other people going to the summit but got unhappy with that role, so jumped ship.

"He had been climbing for only three years. He summited Everest! You get to talking to him and find he's raced sports cars, skydived, all that. A lot of big expeditions wind up in shooting matches; people come back as enemies. We didn't come back enemies, even the guy who left. But it was pretty gross for my wife, Emily, who was one of the Base Camp managers, forced to sit around listening to guys doing farting contests and talking about women as sex objects, which depressed her. On the other hand, I had some real interesting conversations where I learned a lot from some of the people on the expedition.

"After you've been climbing on the world's highest mountain, what are you going to follow that with? Maybe you're better off trying to understand the subconscious, non-logical things that happen on mountains, and trying to become more sensitive to what's going on there. That flies in the face of the culture's belief that mountains are just hunks of rock and ice.

"We need to be sensitive about impinging on other people's places. There's a spirit-quest place the Colvilles have on Leona or Copper Butte, on the Kettle crest, and I think we need to be careful about impinging on those places, on burial grounds and such. But I think we ought to be sensitive about mountains themselves. Other than that, I don't like seeing limits put on human goals. Except, I would temper that by saying that just because we can do something doesn't mean we should. Our culture has proven that point in spades.

"I want to continue to grow as a person. I don't think I'm much of a Type A anymore. I don't feel any need to get truckloads and trainloads of stuff; you know: 'he who dies with the most toys wins'. He who dies with the most toys still dies. I think about building a new house – as much for the experience of building as about living in it. Somehow, after building our cabin, there's a personality in it. People who have some kind of connection walk in and say, 'This feels good.' It's a log shack, frankly.

"A lot of people told me when I first got back from Everest that I looked a lot younger. I've pondered that, because I was supposed to look a lot older. Beforehand, I halfway expected the trip would rejuvenate me, in the face of evidence that it would do the opposite. I don't understand what happened; but the older I get, the less I know. I didn't expect to be in this place at this stage of my life but, somehow, I think it's that feeling that keeps me younger and younger as I get older.

"I don't know what it is I want to do now. I'm waiting for the command, if you will: the Puppet Master is going to tell me one of these days. Not a thunderclap, but a still realisation."

MARGINS

Frost margins –
the black cattle a massed shadow
beneath the ridge and
its sirrus of sheep.
Dawn writes itself a poem in
moonset's ripple over
the Sound of Sleat, day
shivering to shore.

STANDING IN PLACE

My first home in Scotland was in a hostel in Flodigarry, at the north end of the Isle of Skye. I lived like a troll under the stairs in a tiny closet of a room, but was happy to call Flodigarry home, grateful for a nook of my own.

I worked for several seasons at the hostel, spending six months there each year and six months on the mountain in Washington. Shifting back and forth each year created, not a sense of balance, but of extremes. Reclusive vs what felt like living in a train station; primitive vs modern; self-employed vs working for a boss; a land of temperature extremes, big wildlife, brief Caucasian history, and great stillness vs a land of middling temperatures, big weather, ancient Caucasian history, and the constant sound and movement of wind and sea.

The worse the weather got on Skye, the cheerier seemed the locals. Almost a satisfaction with how bad things could get: forces beyond control. "Terrible out!" a drenched old woman declared as she climbed on the Staffin bus. Then flashed a feral grin at me. "Crackin' weather," a dripping youth sardonically announced at the next stop.

"Ach, a mere zephyr," Gavin, the hostel owner, would scoff as I vainly tried to hold my ground in 70 mph winds. We hiked through gales, assaulted by horizontal rain, clambering over spongy moors overlooking seas mightily piling against headlands. Gavin, a Highland Councillor, would stride ahead through bog and burn, declaiming about politics and history and local architecture while I lurched behind trying to keep from being blown off the path or sucked into peat-dark oblivion.

"Of course!" I'd say when Gavin asked if I'd like to go for a wee walk. I'd hastily layer-up in most of the clothes I owned while he waited outside in shorts and turned-down kilt socks.

I often sought the moors and sea cliffs, and the maze of rocky spires, crags and plateaus called the Quiraing, to escape the hostel's bustle and my nook's claustrophobia. The end of April 1999 brought glorious weather on Skye. I hiked into the Quiraing, climbing hills cambered with sheep paths, occasionally coming on bits of bone, clumps of shed wool, golden-eyed flowers in the green pelt of the braes. Above reared the gnawed cliffs of the Quiraing. I climbed, then rested in the heather, falling asleep in sunshine with my hat over my face.

Waking, angling higher, I topped a steep hill, shedding jacket and shirt to be cooled by a north-east breeze off the sea. Light flooded the land, glinting on mirror-still lochans, gliding buzzards. Far below were the toy crofts of Flodigarry; I could see ewes camped around Janet's yard; could see Murdie, unaccustomedly wee, escorting cattle into their pasture; toy cars noiselessly cruised the winding ribbon of road. The only sounds were birds – crow, lark, finch and the occasional accordion note of a sheep's bleat.

But edging this revealed landscape, instead of vivid sea, was dense mist. The sea was invisible beneath it. Flodigarry Island erased except for its highest questing tip. Sunlight lay over all the land; lighted mist over all the sea. From where I stood it was as though Skye floated atop a fairy cloud.

Notions of atmospheric enchantment aside, Skye is no Brigadoon. It amazed me how I could hike into a wild-looking landscape, sit down thinking I was at last alone, and moments later hear the swish of nylon windpants and see…tourists. With so much open, treeless land, the walker is exposed. I became more and more cunning in my choices of routes and destinations, driven by a need to be out on the land and alone.

Contrarily, when among people in the hostel I was lonely. My son phoned me from the States one day – unexpected voice from a distant life. It took a few minutes of conversation to recover my identity: mother, known entity, someone with personal history, intimate relationships, kin, a house, shared verbal shorthand, open affections. It felt strange talking about the garden, the dog, the firewood supply, while around me tourists jabbered in half a dozen languages. Outside, an ocean clearly separated me from that other reality; submerged, sealed behind the surface of how I am perceived here, the assumptions, latitudes of relationship.

During November of 1998 I was house-sitting in Flodigarry for Gavin, and woke one morning to the unmistakable roar of a gale. Wind shrieked, ripping along at over 100mph. Rain slashed, gusts flattening and flaying wave-tops in smoking sheets of spume, hypnotic from the snug safety of the house. All day, unyielding. It is extraordinary when air takes command; like the impact of falling into water from a great height – something you expect to give way suddenly clobbers you like a concrete block.

Periodically I ventured outside to check that the hostel roof tiles and gutters were holding. It was brutal, that wind -- impossible to stand in it. Trees began snapping. Not just branches but whole trunks. The howl of the wind through the small wood was appalling. Gavin's polytunnel began to destruct.

Something had to be done. The hostel warden and I went to work with hammers, re-battening the heaving, flapping plastic, dismantling the overhead water pipes, staggering and clutching for stability as the wind slammed us around. We sawed and dragged broken trees from the driveway. Rain stung like flung gravel. Branches hurtled through the air. At dusk, just before a tour bus arrived at the hostel, the power went out. We lit candles, got the travellers settled; for them a memorable Highland adventure.

I realised afterward that for the first time in months I felt purely myself. Living at the hostel with its electricity, phone, TV, cash register, fax; surrounded by transients; I was an alien, my skills and knowledge unused. But candles for lighting? Totally familiar. Elemental extremes? Bring 'em on. A hard confession, but I find Hebridean weather magnificent. More sun, less wind, fewer midges and the Highlands would be most people's idea of paradise. Imagine indolent West Harris beach resorts, hideaway luxury chalets in Knoydart, dude ranches in Bettyhill, condos around Gairloch, Scourie, Loch Maree….

Bless Scottish weather.

In July of 1999 I moved out of the hostel – where even on a lucky night I'd get only 3-4 hours sleep; where communal living was making me neurotic (one night when a drunk hosteler fell down the stairs above me at 4 am, I shook my fist at the ceiling and hissed "Die, Aussie!"). Norma, my workmate who lived with her husband Neil on one of the Flodigarry crofts, took pity and invited me to live in a caravan on the croft.

My new abode had survived a succession of inhabitants and a winter gale that had lifted and flipped it. Windows and doorframes were still a bit askew, but the caravan's location provided a generous view of Nicolson sheep, the sea, Flodigarry Island and the mainland coast tipped by the nightly wink of Gairloch's lighthouse. The July hills were deep in flowers, croft houses gleamed; inland reared the Quiraing. For company I could nip down to Norma's, often encountering her sister-in-law, or Neil home from the sea, or the three grandsons visiting on weekends, or one of the three grown and gone daughters.

Summer life in the caravan was idyllic: soft, lush; sweeps of wind. During storms the caravan quivered and strained like a moored boat. On calmer days I'd sit on the stoop, gazing down to the shore, colours shifting, shifting, in the north's pure play of light; cool hues you could drink.

Visitors dropped by, duly commented upon by my neighbours. I'm not much of a curtain puller after so many years in isolation, so had to get used to passers-by checking on what I was up to inside. Lines of sight between crofts formed a web of knowledge. Collies criss-crossed in their own patterns of interaction; visual, vocal and visitational. Gregarious sentries.

Flitting to the caravan caused shifts in my community standing. I was now under Norma's auspices instead of Gavin's; my bus stop now at the crofters' turnoff instead of the hostel driveway. Not much change, physically measured, but a significant closing of social distances, though it would be delusional to imagine becoming an insider – not an acquired position in the Highlands. Norma did her best for me, and though I now live at the other end of Skye, visits to Norma are like homecomings.

During my final season at Flodigarry, when my husband and I were both staying at the caravan, we met a young couple who were working at the hotel. The man was South African, the woman Swedish, and we got to know them through their interest in climbing. They worked the tourist season at the hotel, saving money, and went on spectacular outdoor adventures on the off-season. Pakistan, Nepal, Africa, South America, Antarctica. The more remote the better. They didn't want amenities, comforts, tours, frills. They wanted as direct an interface as possible with indigenous cultures and extreme landscapes, wanted their own capacities to be ucompromisingly challenged and to learn how to be "with" natural places.

They walked their talk, right enough, and were impressively fit, physically and emotionally, for these kinds of ventures. I liked them for their passion, and as people. But it gave me food for thought – this travelling to remote places to both test yourself against and surrender yourself to the wild. This driven search for somewhere unspoiled, some hunter-gatherer type people who would demonstrate ancestral wisdom about connection and survival.

At one time I may've longed for this same experience, but lacked this couple's energy and focus (and physiques). As I accumulated perspective from Native people in the States, and experience of my own living "on the land", I found much of that longing fulfilled without having to look beyond my own home.

In the process I became sensitised to "wilderness" and indigenous peoples, and how quickly – maybe inevitably – "unspoiled" places and cultures are altered for the worse by the most well intentioned seekers. Seekers come and go, taking their photos, memories, experiences; the land and locals remain, living with the consequences.

The South African man, during summers at the hotel, led individuals or parties of visitors on hikes in the Quiraing. By the end of the season he was sick of it. His enjoyment of Flodigarry's landscape was blighted by the tedium of repeating these same walks over and over with a succession of visitors who conflated into one faceless, easily despised entity: Tourist. Irritant and income source.

Locals serving visitors the world over know this feeling. I'm sure our friend knows that locals who guide or are obliged to respond to his presence in their remote fastnesses may also feel this, toward him. No matter how little he asks of them. This is a dilemma for him, wanting to be independent, also wanting to learn. He may earn respect, become an individual in someone's eyes, receive generous welcome. Traditional peoples tend to courtesy – look at the Scots.

But you can't learn how to be with a place, or a society, for that matter, in a visit. You can be changed by a visit, and affect change by visiting, and consider if it's a fair trade.

Our friend knows the landscape of Flodigarry maybe better than the locals, in some ways, and I admire this in him, but he has no commitment to it. Living in Flodigarry, helping Norma on the croft when Neil was away at sea, I got a glimpse of local relationship to place (though Norma, being from Scalpay Harris, doesn't consider herself local; Neil is local).

I helped with the sheep, particularly during the lambing. The caravan was surrounded by sheep that time of year, butting against my walls, the sound of grass ripping as they grazed was the backdrop to my activities. Orphan lambs cavorted, waiting to be bottle-fed. Norma's collie gave birth to her pups on the caravan floor. I felt part of things.

It was troubling, especially as a vegetarian, to know what happens to sheep. And troubling what happens to the land because of sheep. But as an incomer I felt I had no right or inclination to judge. I loved living there, and working with the animals, and with Norma and her neighbours. It was a gift.

One spring evening Norma and I were on the hill feeding the sheep and checking new lambs. Before going back to the house we sat down for a while, watching the sheep feed and settle for the night. Norma spoke of her mother's recent death and about difficulties her daughters were going through. I listened – she wasn't looking for input, just expressing her pain, talking it out a little.

Our view on the hill was of the shore, the sea and islands and mainland beyond. The setting sun behind us illumined headlands and crags – water, sky, and mountains all shades of the same dreamy blue. It was companionable sitting together on an empty feed-sack amid this beauty, the crofts and sheep, the peace of the evening. I may've been getting hungry or chilly; my mind may've wandered, but in the awareness of beauty it was as if the sea listened, the sky, the light and colour, the power of the land brought to bear on the human situation.

After a while Norma broke off to remark, "It's really lovely up here tonight, isn't it." Decades of going up that hill to feed the sheep. Decades of personal hardship, tragedy, sacrifice; sleet in the face, too much to do, a husband at sea, an ill supported, denigrated or romanticised way of life. And she could sit there in the midst of her sorrow and point out how really lovely it was, up there that night.

ISLAND COMES

The island comes toward us as though
it is the boat that is moored.
Lights on either side –
passing liners? – or
a harbour's arms outstretched,
arriving.

SHORES

The elemental hardness of the Western Isles forces the bloom of a certain temperament. A Harris resident once answered a jibe about his island's treelessness by saying, "Why should we need trees – we have nothing to hide."

An islander from adjoining Lewis, when asked the date of his birth, replied, "March the sixth."

"Which year?" his questioner unwisely pressed.

"Every year."

One can see why the Fife Adventurers never got anywhere.

I visited Drinishader, on the Isle of Harris, in December one year. It was cold: north wind, full moon's silver light vacillating on the bay. Roddy met me at the ferry; when I opened the passenger door of his work van a spanner slid off the seat, clanging to the pavement, a homey sound. At the hostel he kneed the red sofa closer to the stove, swinging open sooty doors to rouse the coal fire. We slouched on the sofa, feet propped on the stove doors. "Were you out on the sea during that last gale?" I asked, recalling hundred mph wind. Roddy creel-fished.

"No thanks these days," he shrugged. "Too old for it. Used to be I'd go out in weather like that just to be out in it; last one in, that kind of thing."

Thirty-five, three kids: his too old lacked conviction. Roddy went to the kitchen, returned with glasses, dividing what remained of a bottle of single malt left by a hostel guest.

"Slainte."

Midnight came and went, Roddy occasionally rolling cigarettes from his package of Drum, fingers moving with a seaman's economy, going outside to smoke and periodically refill the coal bucket. Drinishader hunkered in rocky abidance under the moon's silent spectacle. Roddy's family has been on Harris since the 1600s. His father and grandfather had been fishermen; Roddy and his two brothers fish. Given the chance Roddy would nonchalantly head out around the world in a boat; someone his ancestors would easily recognize.

An unwordy man, devotedly self-employed. His first boat, the seventeen-foot clinker-built "Otter" was acquired for fifty quid when Roddy was nineteen. I probed him about fishing's specialised vocabulary. He obliged, defining pelagic. "What do you call fish that feed on the bottom?" I asked, ready for more esoterica.

"Bottom-feeders."

The previous year I came in from an early walk through Drinishader. It was June – daylight until nearly midnight, then dawn two hours later. No one was around as I walked. An enclosing misty rain increased the deception of isolation, of removal from outside history or future. Treeless, relentlessly, acidly rocky, nothing on Harris appears to have arisen from ordinary cycles of growth and decay; time bound to the long inhale and exhale of stone and sea. These notions gripped me, though were not ones I imagined shared by Drinishader's own people, used to the island's rhythms.

The Outer or Western Isles are the westernmost reach of Europe. The cultural roots are Gaelic and Norse; the area remains the Gaelic language's stronghold in Scotland. But the population of the Western Isles has been inexorably declining for some time. Difficult social and economic conditions.

Outsiders consider the Western Isles remote, perhaps quaint – or boring – but anyway a place and culture on the edge. This view's double and possibly contradictory emphasis is on bringing in tourism capitalising on the native culture - and on importing mainstream jobs and culture. Despite this, what I see when visiting Roddy is centredness, not fringe-dwelling. Roddy is interested in other places and cultures, but is firm in who and where he is.

His family's four hundred years on Harris may not be long in Scottish terms, but enough that Roddy knows who his people are and where he stands, which is in a Gaelic heartland, not on an edge. Some of how he does things seems naturally linked to tradition, some not. These days traditional sensibilities tend to be dismissed as "trying to turn back the clock." But progress is not a matter of marching forward or turning back (or stagnating). There are old ways that still make sense – socially, spiritually or practically – there are worthwhile evolutions of old ways, and there are visionary new ways. All these could come under the simple heading of good ways to go about things and relate to one another. Forget notions of progress or turning back the clock.

How could we judge what a good way is? Maybe that it avoids waste and harm, promotes congenial relationships and is creatively effective.

Coming back to Roddy, I find in him an instinct for good ways of doing things, that doesn't need to divide traditional and new into separate boxes. He clearly operates from who and where he is – a modern Gael. What if we looked at indigenous culture in its here and nowness? As a referent and well-spring instead of a relic or romance?

As I walked through Drinishader that June evening, drawing close to a house on a rise of ground, I heard the sound of psalm singing like the surge and fall of ocean swell, rolling to crest and break on a mainland fringe.

PART TWO   LANDSCAPE

GNEISS

Rock 3000 million years old –
diggers exhume it, shove it,
tear it naked to thin light.
From peat-black pools
the monster may yet rise,
shudder and break an unwinking surface,
snatch sheep snugged in heather
beside blackwater bogs – what was
before sheep, before names.

SINGING TO THE SEALS

"The notion of magic rests on the idea of a rational universe."
MICHAEL NEWTON

S ummer solstice. Three American friends and I hunker against a sheltering
slab of rock on the Isle of Skye. The ever-blowing Hebridean wind pushes
low whitecaps along the channel between island and mainland; gulls
cruise and wheel above us. Catherine opens her journal notebook and begins
reading aloud in a clear carrying voice:

> *Awaken you lands*
> *All you people out there, live*
> *Live strong*
> *The power is still here*
> *Live strongly and true, you birds*
> *Animals, creeping and swimming ones*
> *Awaken my people*
> *Return to the old ways*
> *It is not too late*
> *Remember, and live again*
> *Live strongly*

This is the vision quest song of our friend Lewis Sawaquat, a Potawatomie
medicine man in the United States. As Catherine begins to read, a grey seal
explodes into view in front of us, close to shore, a large fish flapping in the seal's
powerful jaws. A galvanising moment of interface: life and death, sky and sea.

Catherine takes a deep breath and continues to read. Throughout, a group of
grey seals undulates beneath the translucent surface of the kyle, rolling, gliding,
diving: and when our devotions conclude they disappear like merry sylphs going
off to find the next party.

In the Celtic world there were beings known as selkies who were seals most
of the time, but occasionally took off their pelts to become human beings. Some
stories specify a pattern to this transformation: every ninth night or on certain
full moons, for instance. (The number three and its multiples were mystically
significant.) Some selkies were men; some were women; usually they only

ventured landward as far as offshore or inshore rocks. Seals are reputed to be fond of music, and selkies were said to be inclined to sing as they basked in moonlight on dark, bulking rocks along remote shores. In the Hebrides, local folk would sometimes be deeply and fearfully moved by strange sorrowful music heard out at sea. Music they called the Dan nan Ron (the song of the seals).

The origin of selkies is often attributed to a Norse explanation of the first selkies being the enchanted, transformed children of King Lochlainn. The spell on the clan *(clan righ Lochlainn fo gheasan)* lifted three times a year at full moons. Voluntary shape-shifting and being unwillingly turned into animals, trees, stones, and so on, were classic themes in Celtic (and Norse-Gaelic) stories. Theirs was a very flexible view of embodiment: experience definitive of form rather than vice versa, and experience encompassing a wide spectrum of co-existent realities.

In tales about selkies – of which there are many in Scotland and Ireland – it often happens that an ordinary lonely person, chancing on a selkie in its human aspect, nabs the selkie's seal pelt. The result is that the selkie is not only limited to human form, but is also compelled to remain with the person in possession of the pelt. Selkies were loathe to do this but nonetheless always performed admirably as domestic partners, though there was always something a bit odd about them. Most selkie stories have sad endings for the humans involved – sometimes for the selkies too. No matter how compatible selkie and abductor turn out to be; no matter how close the bond between selkie and offspring; no matter how long the selkie has been in human form; if the pelt can be recovered (as usually happens, eventually) the selkie invariably returns to the sea.

There is an instructive story from the Highlands:

Beautiful Fionagalla and her sister selkies were reclining on the rocks one full moon night, combing their long dark hair and singing to the shiver of moonlight on the sea. Their fair bodies were luminous, their seal pelts dark rumpled heaps like cast-off clothing on the beach. Three brothers came upon the selkies thus, and were seized by desire. They crept close and snatched three pelts, triumphantly gripping them as the selkies eerily cried out and dived like quicksilver into the swaying waves. Three were left, their sad gazes locked upon the pelts tightly clutched by the young men, and Fionagalla was one.

The selkies wept and begged but to no avail; two of the brothers marched their prizes home, leaving Fionagalla facing the third. He looked at her with longing but knew he could not find happiness at such price, so he handed the seal pelt to Fionagalla; she snatched it and instantly was gone.

Days passed; the youth could not put the selkie from his mind. On the ninth night he went to the rocks where he'd first seen her and – yes! – there she was, this time in the company of her father. *"You must thank this man for his kindness, and do rightly by him in return,"* her father told Fionagalla, and so she did. *Accompanying the youth to his home, she spent the night helping him clean and tidy his stone cottage with its modest accoutrements. They made a simple meal together and companionably chatted while they worked. Both of them enjoyed this so much that Fionagalla returned thereafter every ninth night to continue this congenial activity, and they were ever happy.*

Meanwhile the other two brothers sat back and let their selkie wives do all the work of house and croft and raising children. One selkie spouse found her pelt where it had been hidden and promptly vanished with it into the sea. The other one's husband, in a panic at this, tried to burn his wife's pelt. It exploded, setting the house afire; the man escaped but his selkie wife did not, dying in the blaze, far from the ocean's cool embrace.

I found this story in a museum archive, filed among census figures, descriptions of farming techniques, Gaelic names for flowers, lists of clan pipers and so on. This integration of aspects of culture was not an accident of eccentric filing; Celtic culture was woven from such an integration, where ancestors may be deities or Otherworld beings and even more recent relatives may have astonishing bloodlines.

Take the MacCodrums of North Uist, in the Western Isles, for example. There used to be abundant numbers of seals on the rocks of Cousamul and Hasker in MacCodrum's distict. Story has it that a MacCodrum ancestor, Neill, was walking one day on the shores when he observed seals putting off their coverings and bathing in human form. He absconded with one of those pelts and hid it above his door lintel. Its owner was forced to follow. He gave her human garments and married her on the third night, and had a family. Years later, as is generally the case, one of the children found the pelt and gave it to the selkie, who donned it and arrowed back into the sea, singing.

After that, the MacCodrums were known as *clann 'Ic Odrum nan ron* (the MacCodrums of the seals). They were of bardic lineage. John MacCodrum, the most famous, was brought up in the 1700s on a promontory jutting into the western sea near Aird-a-Runair, a burying ground on North Uist. He was poor, didn't read or write, and spoke no English. Though the MacCodrums lived where seals were extensively hunted for their skins (used for horse harnesses) and oil (used for lamps), no MacCodrum would kill seals, eat their meat, or use sealskins or oil.

A communal seal hunt took place every year in late October. A MacCodrum woman used to be gripped by violent pains during this annual hunt. The place where the slain seals were deposited occasionally would be the site of a haunting visitation by a woman sometimes described as old, sometimes described as lovely and young, dressed in a green mantle over which flowed her long yellow hair. The woman, recognising members of her family among the dead seals, would lament: *Spog Fionghall, Spog Fionghall, spog spaidreig, spog spaidreig, spog mo Chuileinn, chaoimh chaidrich.*

The MacCodrums were bards to the MacDonalds of Sleat. John MacCodrum's satires had wit and banter, though were never coarse. He fathered only one child, a daughter Mary. The family emigrated to Canada in the 1800s – none of the MacCodrum lineage remain in the Isles. It was suggested that some of the MacCodrums could and did assume seal shape at times, and several lost their lives that way. The bard John was short and broad, thick-set, with a pale complexion, brown hair and eyes.

The MacCrimmons of Skye and the MacPhees of Colonsay, also in the Hebrides, claimed seal descent; such families were known as *sliochd nan ron*. Other Highland families were linked with animal totems: the MacKelvies with doves, the MacMasters with pigs, the MacGregors with bloodhounds, the MacLeods with horses, the MacDonalds with dogs, and the MacIntoshes, MacNichols and MacNeishes with cats.

The sea is a realm the Celts considered a portal or path to the Otherworld. All kinds of strange beings are in the sea and all kinds of strange things happen there. In Celtic countries – especially in the isles – the sea is a realm where countless Gaels journey, make their livelihoods, and die. Celtic customs and attitudes toward the sea continue to exist in remnant form.

In the old days, before setting sail, prayers of protection (called urnaigh mhara) were recited by Hebridean fishermen, in the form of chants. After calling out three blessings on the boat (beannaicht an long), a characteristic (post-pagan) chant involved the helmsman asking what is to be feared with God the Father/the Son/and Spirit watching over them. The crew would reply in unison: "We will fear nothing at all". The helmsman would then ask, what could give them anxiety with the God of the elements/the King of the elements/the Spirit of the elements watching over them; to which the crew would reply, "No anxiety can be ours" (*Cha churam dhuinn ni*).

In Scotland you never stand more than fifty miles from the ocean; the sea pervades, ever a force to be reckoned with. Fishermen and sailors still make their quiet propitiations and heed certain taboos. But what did it really mean to be of the *sliochd nan ron*? When I wrote to the editor of a magazine on shamanism, asking if he would be interested in an article about selkies, he replied that I'd have

to approach the subject carefully because biological cross-insemination between seals and humans is impossible; therefore, having seal lineage would be a folk metaphor for having shamanic abilities, not really biological descent from seals.

Pondering this reply, I realised that while I don't particularly disagree with this view, neither do I consider it particularly pertinent. Whether or not the sliochd nan ron had seal blood in a biological sense, that is not the lens through which selkies can be seen and understood, any more than is proof or disproof of a Loch Ness monster a definitive basis for understanding a people's relationship with habitat. The Celts knew embodiment's essential insecurity of tenure; that life moves in transformative cycles. They expressed this understanding in myriad ways, including their distinctive artwork: a flow of shifting forms, abstraction resolving into tree, becoming stag, turning to human, never static.

There is nothing fanciful in the Celts' acceptance of the way form shifts, life feeding into life; quantum physics has this same recognition, in less poetic terms. But both recognise how relationship continually influences form in a cohesive universe. The legendary shaman Tuan O'Cairell of ancient Ireland said, with concrete authority of experience, "I passed into the shape of a river salmon…was vigorous and well-fed and my swimming was good, and I used to escape from every danger and from every snare − to wit, from the hands of fishermen, and from the claws of hawks, and from the fishing spears − that the scars with which each of them left are still on me." (John Matthews. *Taliesin*. The Aquarian Press; London, 1991, p. 161)

The MacCodrums had a distinct relationship with seals − a hereditary relationship. They were a bardic family; perhaps some of them had and used shamanic abilities. The Celts didn't need to separate metaphor from biology, indeed saw the danger of doing so, as much wisdom would be lost in the process. In the Hebrides it was commonly put forth that once taking on a seal form a person could no longer return to being an ordinary dry-land person. Once mundane limitation is relinquished for knowledge of the Otherworld, there is no return to ignorance. But selkies did, at times, and under compulsion, live on land. There is an old Irish story that offers a perspective:

Declan, an Irishman of the coast, spent the morning catching cockles and crabs on the beach, and lay down a while to rest. Strange music woke him; sitting up he saw twelve people − six couples − swaying and singing in a circle on the beach, an old man in their midst. In a heap on a stone lay a shimmering pile of "cloaks" these people had cast aside in their dance.

The couples soon went off separately to make love, leaving their cloaks behind. Declan darted to the stone and seized one of the beautiful cloaks, thinking to sell it in the village. No sooner did he have it in hand than the couples returned, and Declan quickly ducked behind the stone on which the coverings lay. He watched as one by one the cloaks were reclaimed and the people, whom Declan now realised were seal people, slithered into the water.

One woman remained. Searching for her cloak she discovered Declan and, extending her delicately webbed hand, asked for what was hers. Declan, jerking out his knife and waving it at the seal woman, demanded he be given something in exchange. "We are the last of the Ron," the woman said, still unafraid; "the people banished to the waves. Every hundred years we come ashore to conceive children who are able to move freely between land and sea, between human and seal form,"

Declan lunged at the seal woman, determined in his hostility to take his pleasure with her. She cried out and from the waves rushed a bull-seal who struck Declan with his flippers and sank sharp teeth into his leg. The woman pulled her cloak from Declan's grasp and in a flash both selkies were gone. One summer later, Declan ventured too far out at low tide in search of crabs; he slipped on a wet kelpy rock and was drowned.

Lineage was of central importance to Celts. In all arenas, continuity functioned through kinship that included fosterage as well as direct bloodlines. People tended to follow hereditary occupations: bardic lineages, families of boat builders, pipers, stone-carvers, physicians, and so on. Government structures were kin-based; law focused on communal responsibilities. Most telling of all, perhaps, the Celts believed themselves the descendants of deities, an integration of mortal humans, elemental forces and supernatural beings. In view of such antecedents, it is not surprising to find families claiming seal kin or descent from clans banished to the sea.

Identity came through relationship; the ultimate punishment was not death but ostracism. A perspective of selkies as being only a folk metaphor for shamanic ability does not seek far enough into cultural realities.

I was hiking on the moors one dreich day on the northwest coast, near Gairloch. Water-kelpies were said to inhabit many of the area's lochs, particularly one at Greenstone Point. Off Port Henderson, across the bay from where I was walking, a mermaid had once been captured by young Roddy MacKenzie, who exacted a promise from her that no one would ever drown from a boat Roddy made. His boats became legendary, and no one ever drowned from one. The waters of nearby Loch Maree traditionally were considered healing, one of its isles a fairy place. But the most famed of the area's fairies, during the 1700s, was the Gille Dubh of Loch a Druing, which lies a couple of miles from where I was hiking that day. He was a beneficent fairy, the ally of a young girl named Jessie MacRae, but for some (probably Calvinist) reason, a party of gentry rode out to try and shoot the fairy. After that the Gille Dubh understandably kept a low profile.

The day I was hiking, a seal's head broke the surface of the water below a high headland I was wandering. The seal looked up, studying me in curious seal fashion, then began to criss-cross the cove. Seized by an urge to explore the cove's beach, I clambered down the cliff, dropping the final sheer yards in a knee-jarring freefall to the cobbles below. It was a place of kelp-slick red boulders, weirdly sculpted caves, and towering sea stacks. The seal tolerated my company for a time, then vacated the cove. When mist resolved into rain I started back up the steep slope. High above the cove I paused to rest, sheltering beneath an overhang of stone, a narrow crevice at my back. From this small dark crack in the slope streamed a chill cave-like draught, as though the land exhaled from deep in its body.

I sat wedged against rock, rain stippling the ocean below, water dripping from the stone eave. I grew cold in this motionless pose, but tarried in a kind of elementally hypnotised contentment. This was broken by an abrupt loud sound, seeming to come from within the slope, distinctly like the slam of a door, and with that the chill draught of air behind me ceased.

This felt both startling and not. It didn't matter whether the noise had been a natural phenomenon or the Gille Dubh closing the door to the Otherworld. The compulsion to lunge for beliefs, disbeliefs, and explanations is often the antithesis of clarification.

Stories about selkies are tales of primal fluidity within encounters emphasising choices and their consequences. Those tales suggest that mystery will reappear again and again with its allure, beauty we so often either fear or want to grasp and control, domesticate. But again and again mystery escapes us unless we respect its intrinsic integrity. Intrinsic integrity is the opposite of forced marriage, and what we grasp eventually will be loosed by the consequences – the selkies' offspring – of bondage.

The interface of what is wild and what is humanly governed was conceded by Celts to be a perilous experience. That some of the MacCodrums reportedly lost their lives while in the form of seals suggests that if it is futile to domesticate mystery, it is also risky to venture into its own precinct. In Celtic tradition no moral dissuasion about interaction with the Otherworld was imposed, but relationship tended to be canny.

Celtic sennachies recited tales in winter, at night, much as did American Indian storytellers. Otherworld doings were best approached at times when they wouldn't be stirred into disrupting the mundane business of day. To name was to invoke. People were wary of how these forces infiltrated life and could turn the ordinary on its ear. Coexistent realities are taken for granted as present, for people who live with the elements in their faces; they avoid complacency.

There is a famous song, *The Selkie of Sule Skerry* in which a male selkie seduces a land woman and she becomes pregnant. Before going back to the sea the selkie tells the woman that she will wed a gunner and the gunner will shoot the selkie, which is of course what happens seven years later when the selkie returns for his son. A haunting song full of inevitability, sex, love, lament, the dance of choice and fate. I also heard a version of an old Gaelic chant to the seal women, that used to be sung in the Western Isles. The songs have endured – there may be something still to be learned from the relationships which engendered them.

HEBRIDEAN ECONOMY

On the news they're talking global slowdown
but it's not happening here;
the wind – MY GOD – spinning us faster;
I'm clutching doorframes
to keep the centrifugal force
from sucking me right out the house.

AN AMERICAN IN GAELDOM

Hawks wheel over the mountain, wingtips carving spirals in the blue air.
Moving runes pattern the land; tree shadows, massed cloud migrations. Sunset saturates
the patient ground, disappears. I wake in the night, the thread of
remembrance growing tenuous as I drift from what I know.

I wrote this when I moved to the Isle of Skye. Coming from a decade on the mountain, I had to learn a different way of life. One with electricity, indoor toilets, telephones…people. Tourists find Skye rustic. It is not so for me; it is emphatically modern. But there is an ancestral pattern in how Gaels coexist with the land and one another that feels grounded in collective sensitivity. This quality is not always merciful, but it is aware, thus responsive. What culturally exists on Skye is a way of life defined, often occluded, by encounters with feudalism, clearances, anglicisation, and global consumerism. Yet, in certain everyday ways, it remains Celtic.

My sense of this may be strongly influenced by my initial two years on Skye being in Flodigarry, a crofting community of Gaels. Only once in my years in Skye – north and south – have I witnessed a disintegration of native courtesy, and that was when a local bus driver, badgered by a passenger, exploded when casually insulted with, "Can't you understand English?"

It is a touchy thing, this matter of Gaelic, locked within the push-pull of Highland pride and shame. Gaelic has enemies, still, and many people indifferent to the language's survival. Indeed, why should modern Scots care about Gaelic? Where is its relevance to non-Gaelic lives, to the country's overall future? Why should Gaelic-speaking parents, even, press for language policies that may contribute nothing toward their children's "getting on" in today's world?

But Gaelic, unlike Babylonian and other ancient languages, has endured as a spoken tongue. Transformed over the centuries, of course, but still here, as Gaels, also transformed, are still here. That astonishing longevity itself should provoke consideration. The notion of monolingual nations is new. Scotland has always been multicultural, multilingual. There's no reason a Scot necessarily should identify with Gaelic or with Celtic culture (whatever that may be). But Gaelic is the voice of a unique species of Scottish human beings, and though not every Scot is a Gael, every Highland Gael is a Scot. Gaels and Gaelic are intrinsic to the consciousness that is Scotland. Loss of that is cultural amnesia, impoverishing the resources of the Scottish whole, and the whole's future.

In the cities, noticeably, many children attending Gaelic play-schools or Gaelic-medium classes are not from Gaelic-speaking families, a development mirroring the increase in adult Gaelic learners who are not native Highlanders – or, indeed, Scottish. This situation raises questions about the relationship between language and culture. If Gaels themselves stop speaking Gaelic, what context will the language have? What relevance? What will it be communicating besides an English or Danish or American mindset translated into Gaelic vocabulary?

At one point in a conversation with a man on Harris, as he rummaged through his Gaelic mind for an appropriate English noun, I suddenly was chagrined at taking for granted the conversation in English. It was his courtesy in the face of dozens of similar daily presumptions, a dematerialising of culture in its own house. The previous year he had remarked, "My kids feel like part of a prehistoric society when they use Gaelic."

One of the taxi drivers on Skye told me about growing up in the north part of Skye, of going to work on the sea and spending most of his life there, as many Isle men do. Made redundant, he now drives a taxi. He speaks Gaelic. "Do your daughters?" I asked, and he shook his head: regret, but not as though there had been expectations.

For him Gaelic is simply part of his local landscape of social relations. I doubt he views it as something he should feel culturally obligated to perpetuate. And as with many Gaelic-speaking parents, it is their children's manifest interest in Gaelic that determines whether the language is taken up. Transmission of Gaelic is not "bothered with" if children – (ostensibly) due to some bent of individual nature – shun it. Of course, individual nature is influenced by ubiquitous English/American TV in the heart of Highland households, peer pressure, and a deterring image in larger society.

At one of the piping recitals I attended at Sabhal Mòr Ostaig, the Gaelic college at the southern end of Skye, the programme began by showcasing an American who runs a piping school in the States. His presentation was graciously applauded. Taking a break from the onslaught of pibroch, we enjoyed Christine Primrose's Gaelic singing, the audience joining in on choruses.

The recital closed with Angus MacColl, a gold medallist from Argyll. As the formal music approached conclusion, Angus suddenly succumbed to hotdogging, using wrists and the sides and backs of his fingers and hands in a display of

Pacific rattlesnake on First Thought Mountain

Golden mantle squirrel, Bend, Oregon

Turtles in California

Coyote in NE Washington state

Our house on First Thought Mountain

Applecross beach, northwest Highlands

Raiding bear, First Thought Mountain

Garter snake, First Thought Mountain

breakneck piping panache. As the last impeccable note skirled, the crowd went – by pibroch recital standards – wild.

This is not a defeated people.

Gaelic's situation has greatly improved since the early 1980s when only a hundred of the pre-schoolers in Scotland spoke the language, but it will be a while before increases in Gaelic-medium playgroups and school classes have an observable effect on Highland society. No way of telling, for example, whether learning Gaelic will encourage people to stay in or return to Highland areas. (Between 1849 and 1880, 83,000 people left Skye; the island's current population stands at around 9,000, a fifth of them born in England.)

In the Western Isles there are about equal numbers of children in Gaelic-medium and English-medium education. Strengthening local economies in rural areas might strengthen the use of Gaelic. Despite the fact that most Gaelic preservation efforts over the past thirty years have been governmentally sponsored, local community support for and use of the language is the crux.

Finlay MacLeod, chief executive of Gaelic play-school playgroups, related a story about addressing in Gaelic a kilted man encountered on Skye. The man responded by demanding, "Why are you speaking to me in that foreign language?"

Finlay explained that he'd taken the kilt as cue.

"I'm proud to be Scottish," the man retorted, "I wear the kilt every day. It has nothing to do with Gaelic."

As Finlay's story made clear, Gaelic has little to do these days with Scottish identity. Gaelic learners do not have an easy road between general prejudice against the language and a degree of native-speaking prejudice against learners. More than a few native speakers have declared that they'd rather see the language die than have it become what they feel is artificial or hobbyist: something belonging to universities and faddish outsiders, an indignity no longer organic to rural lives. Such people are wary of preservation tactics regarded as gimmicky. With few exceptions, the Gaelic revival in Scotland has not displayed the militancy or grassroots fervour seen in parallel ethno-national movements.

Language preservation – even if successful – won't necessarily include Gaelic cultural preservation or renewal. Not if the language becomes orphaned from its rural roots and the worldview and way of life it encodes – things that are not being transmitted to academic learners along with the grammar.

Dr Wilson MacLeod, former teacher at Sabhal Mòr Ostaig, reacted to my interest in what's going on with Gaelic by saying, "If you want to talk to Gaelic speakers, go to Edinburgh; that's where Gaelic is happening, not in the Highlands and Islands."

I was entirely put-off by this statement with its reinforcement of the impression that native-speaking Gaeldom is being written-off by academia. Later, during a more sympathetic conversation with Wilson, he sharply criticised the way government money for Gaelic goes to superficial tokens instead of needy projects such as creation of a Gaelic thesaurus and a standard grammar text. "Ireland has had Gaelic secondary schools for decades; where are the Scottish ones?" he asked.

A good question, but the problem is not just a matter of schools. How many of the Irish actually use Gaelic in daily life? Estimates are low – 10,000 perhaps? It is a matter of use it or lose it, and use had to go beyond schools into literature, music, popular media, government, church, workplace, and, most of all, family and community. Into the pubs and hills, not just the hothouse of education. The consensus seems to be that this is unlikely to happen in Scotland. But when you reflect on the thousands of years of Gaelic's evolution and survival, you may be tempted to think: it could.

Inhabitants of the Isles, whatever their language partisanships, continue to ponder what to do for employment: needs for mobility and high costs of petrol, haulage and ferry transport; social problems associated with isolation: paucity of essential services, distances from decision-making, school centralisations taking the young away from home and community – launching them on courses for urban or foreign horizons. Eighteen percent of Skye's population is over sixty-five years old.

Incomers to the Isles tend to be older, richer, English-speaking, and seasonally present, buying settings for their personal fantasies, having disproportionate impacts on local economic and environmental conditions. Problematic foreign-owned business operations dominate the scene: many of these corporations have no commitment to Scotland or to Scottish workers – corporations giveth; corporations taketh away.

As in many rural areas in the world (American Indian reservations come to mind) where sparse, less than affluent native populations are confronted with apparent conflict between environmentalism and employment, dilemmas ensue. Expediency urges make money, bugger ecology, though the corporate hit-and-run attitude is usually masked by a PR message along the lines of: date rape ain't really rape.

But there is no *intrinsic* dichotomy between livelihood and environmental common sense. When common sense is not used – as in the case of North Sea fishing, for example – livelihood is ultimately lost. You saw off the branch you're living on when you ignore environmental reality.

For the Highlands and Islands to thrive neither as an open-air museum nor a hinterland for testing and dumping hazardous materials, the old community pact with the land needs to be renewed. Inhabitants of places where there have been community buy-outs of large estates are attempting this renewal of felicitous relationship with land. Historically, Gaels did not regard land as a commodity. Meg Bateman, who teaches at Sabhal Mòr Ostaig, says in a paper on the subject:

> Nature is not seen as an object outside or different from the human environment. Nature is the human environment, and human settlement is as much a part of it as other forms of life. In short, people are part of nature and nature is part of people…Celtic understanding of a symbiotic relationship between man and nature is the basis of modern ecological thought.

Meg calls this relationship "…a sense of creative engagement with the landscape." Creative engagement is affiliated, intimate, participatory, rather than presumptuous or passive. Challenging rather than adversarial. The difference between the two is subtle but profound; the difference between Gaels and empire-builders. Reclamation of this integrated perspective is not a matter of turning back the clock. On the Isle of Eigg the community buy-out was accomplished in a forward-looking partnership with the Scottish Wildlife Trust and the Highland Council, supporting a framework for human community as a natural, prospering part of island ecology.

There is a vital difference between "jobs" and a way of life. Money as sole objective creates sour societies, undermining values and activities that sustain satisfying relationships.

In the realm of Highland employment, 25% of natural heritage work is located in the Highlands and Islands. Major industries such as whisky distilleries – not to mention ordinary citizens – depend on clean water, so natural heritage workers do more than just preserve our postcard scenery. That scenery is the main reason visitors come to the Highlands and Islands. Our economy relies on tourism, as was recently highlighted by the economic impact of the (non-Highland) foot and mouth crisis: and keeping the scenery presentable is essential to tourism.

But the Highlands can't compete with midge-less sunny Caribbean tour deals, or even European petrol prices. A holiday in the Highlands costs 20% more than in other parts of Europe. Virtually everything from camera film to a night's lodging is cheaper in Europe and North America. The fate of tourism in the Highlands is inseparable from rural issues of land reform, environmentalism and economic policy.

Scotland relies on its romantic image to attract visitors: the power of its landscape; the country's allure to emigrant descendants; its music and antiquities. As an American living in Scotland, and as a seasonal employee in the tourist industry – first in a hostel, now in a gift shop – I am acutely aware of tourists from both a resident's and an outsider's viewpoints. Skye during off-season has a relaxed atmosphere: small events, pub sessions, socialising, quiet roads. Summer's approach brings a closing of ranks and visages, a bracing as rental cars begin congesting the single-track roads, buses disgorge peripatetic backpackers, and winter-starved cash registers again ring.

In 2002 the £60 million "Spirit of Loch Lomond" development opened: a National Park visitor centre expected to draw more than a million yearly users. The facility features a theatre, luxury hotel, orienteering centre, and numerous upscale shops and restaurants. In 1999 the then Scottish tourism minister, Henry McLeish, sounded delighted about the development; I was disquieted. Does Scotland really need more imported polarisation between the rich and not-rich, between visitor and resident? Will servicing the wealthy raise Highland confidence and nourish self-esteem in the young? Will the bonny banks become an elite playground instead of a landscape inviting to all? Is a glitzy consumer attraction the way to celebrate commitment to natural heritage? Does this trend of seasonal minimum-wage work for locals, watching their countryside turn into a resort, make anyone uneasy?

As an employee at a visitor centre I know the uncertainties of pinning your economic fate to such a capricious industry. And I know the difficulties of low wage, seasonal work. Perhaps too many eggs are being placed in the tourist basket.

I recall back in 1988, bringing my mother and son to see Scotland. My mother was particularly taken by the sight of antiquities unannounced by road signs or site plaques, sitting off in fields, part of the landscape. This was back before Eilean Donan had floodlights or Skye had a bridge. Past and present abided in ordinary communion, with the resulting (maybe false) impression that heritage was interwoven with the people's present rather than finished and packaged for foreign consumption. The impact of this is like the difference between jobs and a way of life. There is something whole (and Gaelic) about an integrated concurrency. Regardless of history's tragedies. Or maybe because of them. The past still belongs to the people's relationship with place. In fact, without that, there is a disconnection, an amnesia cutting us off at the roots.

When a stone circle or fortress ruin acquires a car park, a parade of tour buses, a visitor centre selling tartan knick-knacks, it becomes an item for tourists, not a place belonging to the people – or the land. Perhaps this should not trouble me so.

And yet…riding the north Skye bus past the crofts one day, shearers were working in one of the fanks. An unremarkable island scene – except for the bevy of camera-clicking visitors who pulled off the road to capture close-ups of island life in action. Some way down the road, a man pointed a video camera at a ruminating Highland cow. Gaelic conversation on the bus ceased as we trundled past these vignettes, then talk resumed. On Orkney a farmer stomped out to his field and pulled down a neolithic standing stone, fed up with tourist intrusion.

What if locals start selling tickets to shearings, peat cuttings, grain stookings, as they do sheepdog trials and Highland Games? What if visitors start needing a ticket to have a dram in Dougie MacLean's pub? What happens when a people's sense of their lives vacillates between that of an anthropological exhibit and a struggling modern backwater? "Say something in Gaelic," the visitor demands. Life as performance. A language beaten out of schoolchildren within living people's memory.

Out on Harris a postmistress wryly spoke of the way tourists regard the Western Isles as the primitive edge of nowhere. "They seem to think we sit here with nothing to do, waiting for some outsider to bring us a taste of worldly culture." Visitors expect locals to jump at a chance to be of service. "They're surprised we have anything else to do," said the postmistress. "They're surprised we live in real houses."

In what social reality can Gaels invest confidence in the future? How can rural communities best respond to summer affairs with tourists: romances with one lover in it for the money and the other insisting on misty rusticism (but wanting Sunday buses).

A young man from Ohio checked into the hostel where I worked. Boyishly earnest and intense, he was about to inherit a lucrative investments firm from retiring mentors in the States: a youth with ambitions realised early. He had come to Scotland "because of ancestry" and was visiting notable heritage sites, evincing a righteous dislike of the English, and practising saying "aye" instead of "yes". He asked if there was someone local who could tutor him in Gaelic for a day. Serious business, this assumption of the plaid.

Though nakedly naïve, at heart this young man was little different from any visitor or incomer responding to Scotland's draw for the homesick emigrant descendant. It is easy to become a bit couthy, to imagine solidarity, to thrill to the pipes: Braveheart – yeah! (Aye!). But for most of these visitors there is only ardent longing and the reality of immutable Highland politeness.

As often with Americans in Scotland, their travels are prompted by an inarticulate but insistent inner call. Americans in Scotland, particularly those of Scottish descent, are looking for something that abides nowhere else, but for most it is too late – in their own conditioning and in Scotland itself – to find it. Being tourists, they skim too fast, knowing too little, over-itinerised, scenery-saturated. Like cuckoo eggs hatched in another bird's nest, many descendants of Scots emigrants are ignorant of their people's story, and thus what informs their own cultural present and future. There is a gap where connection should naturally exist, a lack of that materialism – the modern culture of North America – cannot fill.

What do castles, Culloden, the Cuillin, add up to? What's in a surname? How did relationships get so mislaid? Ach – the American Dream! Tourists go home and America closes over their heads again; Scotland the dream.

I think about this, then about how Scots like to ridicule Americans, yet always are baffled about why I, an American, would trade living in America for a place like this. It does my head in.

I've heard locals criticise pipers who busk on the pier, calling it prostitution of Highland culture. Hard to know where to go with this culture thing: where the line is drawn between honouring and exploiting, participating and impersonating, preservation and pretentious irrelevance.

On National Poetry Day in 1999, our Skye writers in residence decided a staid Gaelic reading would do nothing to highlight the art. So, on an October day of strong gales they robustly climbed Sleat's highest hill, co-composing a poem in Gaelic and English as they ascended, and at the top released a copy of the poem – along with other poetry – in the whimsical care of helium balloons.

Descending the hill, the poets next boarded a fishing boat on the Sound of Sleat and had a few drinks before being welcomed ashore at Ornsay. The fishing boat's skipper unlimbered his pipes and played as we stood beside the water, wind whipping, the poet-climbers soaked, the piper wearing his oilskins and wellies, no tartan regalia needed to make the moment right.

Indoors, drams were poured and a reading commenced – backed by electrical slide guitar and synthesiser. A German hiker encountered by the poets on the hill had contributed lines (in German); about the weather, naturally. Those present at the reading invented additional lines, then adjourned to the pub. Who's to say what is corruption of tradition and what is tradition's spirit in moment? A truer concern might be that culture has genuine organic life: roots, branches, flowers, fruit, new seeds.

Scotland has regained its legislature, but what will become of its culture and the culture's commercialisation as grist for the tourist mill? The tourism market is seen as essential in employment-strapped places like the Highlands and Islands, but superimposed on unresolved environmental, social, and political problems, it occupies an uneasy position in community. Is it inevitable that there is a distancing between locals and their heritage when cultural continuity is first smashed, then reconfigured and co-opted by outsiders? Could reclamation of heritage parallel reclamation of land, if community buy-outs continue to challenge feudalism in Scotland?

Crofting plays a crucial role in maintaining rural communities and Gaelic culture, preserving values and an approach to life that represents some of Scotland's finest assets. But where is the real livelihood in crofting, which, by design, is economically restrictive in order to ensure cheap local labour for the lairds? Today, more than seventy percent of Scotland is in agricultural use (sheep outnumbering humans two to one) but only twenty percent of the workforce farms. Mechanisation rules; there are barely a thousand shepherds left in the country.

Information technology is not a cultural solution to unemployment in remote areas, though it may open economic possibilities. What may be overlooked is that you don't revitalise communities based on social relationships by parking individuals in call centres or in front of computer screens all day. Community is built on mutualities, reciprocities and direct interaction with people and place. The way forward is to creatively look at this base and its potentials.

When my sister came to Scotland I went down to Edinburgh to meet her. We rented a car and drove over to Aberdeen-shire, to Inverness-shire, up to

Sutherland and Caithness, criss-crossing the north on the B roads, heading down through Wester Ross, on to Skye, and so on until finishing in Perthshire. We drove the single-tracks, hiked, explored. One day my sister asked, "Where's the wildlife?"

We'd seen deer, sheep, cattle, many birds, wildflowers; but tree plantations rather than natural woodlands, and no large land mammals except deer and domestic beasts. Somewhere, I knew there were badgers, foxes, pine martens, Highland cats; but not in numbers balancing those of available prey.

It has been this way for a long time. People are used to it. They may worry about weather, or terrain, or midges when going into the countryside, but they don't have concerns about wildlife encounters. There is no such threat (or thrill) here; also no prompt to reconsider human place and behaviour in nature.

Hillwalkers, and climbers, and flower fanciers, and birdwatchers, and holiday-makers can blithely roam the countryside as though it were a rural park, which in most ways is what it has become – albeit without mandate. Along with "Where is the wildlife?" may be asked "Where are the natives?" for both are now largely absent.

The less people encounter wildlife the less knowledgeable about essential diversity they become, and the less wise in response to other species. Witness the apprehension about reintroduction of European beavers in Argyll; people up in arms about beavers eating all the salmon – when beavers don't eat fish at all.

Scotland lags behind the rest of Europe – and consumptive North America – when it comes to recycling, energy consciousness, and other "green" strategies, yet has the world's premier potentials for wind and wave energy, and a magnificent history – during the Celtic era – of wise relationship with the land. This included minutely detailed laws regarding resource use, arising from knowledgeable and affectionate self-identification with the land and its life. An intimacy that continued to be expressed by much later Gaels such as the bard Duncan Ban MacIntyre; glimpses of this attitude are evident even now. It wouldn't take much to revitalise that heritage.

People I meet, hearing that I'm now a resident, married to a Scot, often ask "Why Skye?"

It has to do with people and land, a not yet obliterated way of life. Why Skye? I could say because of the Cuillin, the Quiraing, the crofters' cairn at Braes, the pipers' cairn at Duntulm; because of friendships and a local ease, the music and craic; because of a history of seers and singers, poets and pipers, recalcitrant crofters; the magic of Rona or Knoydart across moonstruck waters; the thousand ordinary moments when a locality of land, sea, light and life intimately speak to the mind, the senses, the heart.

Or I can recall my neighbour's answers when asked, "What's that hill called in Gaelic?" "Whose boat is that?" "Is that one of Charlie's sheep?" "Has Helen had her baby yet?" Answers mapping duration and event, the continuing story of neighbourhood.

In Washington my life centred in an evocative state of mind called First Thought Mountain. I can navigate familiar parts of that wilderness in the dark, knowing where rock is stable, the shape and details of the slope, where moisture collects, where grouse congregate and rattlers shelter, where bears carve long territorial gashes in cedars, where a branch will slap my cheek if I don't duck.

On Skye I learn: seasonal and weather patterns and their implications; tidal rhythms infiltrating the body's moods; I can close my eyes and see outlines of coast, islands, mainland heights, croft houses like a dot-to-dot picture connected by racing collies. There is a deep sense of well-being in this process of familiarity. Even for the stranger, the moment has its history.

FIRST THOUGHT MOUNTAIN

The land describes itself to me
in winter, in quiet,
in the way each snowflake
touches it.
Contoured by moonlight,
by clouds filling the low places,
by wind in the heights
taking of the rock, grain by grain.
There is no mistake
in these shapes
that guide the flow of light
like riverbanks, the sky moving
in crevices, along bluffs,
then lying in stillness
upon the fields,
renewing the land
even in winter.

THE FITTING TOGETHER
OF PARTS

T hat's America: even the dogs are armed. In the local general store one day I met a logger who had a bandage around his head and a sheepish look on his face. His dog had shot him. Luckily the canine was a poor marksman – it was a young dog. Man's best friend. An anti-gun bumper sticker – a play on Constitutional words assuring the right to bear arms – promotes a right to arm bears.

Arms, bear and dog were involved in the logger's mishap. The logger was beside his truck working; the dog (in the truck along with a rifle in its gunrack) was stimulated by the arrival of a bear. Dog jostles rifle; logger winged.

When we moved to the mountain a local woman told Robin, "You girls have no business being up there without guns." Since we each had a dog perhaps it's fortunate we didn't heed her assertion. Guns are one way of living around Nature. Living with Nature, though, asks for a less militant approach.

Harmony is defined as "a fitting together of parts so as to form a connected whole; a normal state of completeness and order in the relation of things to each other." A paradigm with sound basis and substantial reward, encompassing everything from molecular activity to interactions among nations. A cosmic choreography, each bit playing its part. Reciprocities, balances, encouragement toward wisdom. The big dance.

Living on the mountain, I didn't expect bears to be tidy, rattlers to be cuddly, deer not to get their throats torn out by cougars. I didn't assume my cats and dog would be safe or should have free rein to harry or kill wildlife. I considered the dangers to myself and Gabriel; and that we would have an impact on what was already living there. Everything has impact: the idea was to fit in as best we could.

Creatures came and went from the house – bats, rodents, flying squirrels, bears, frogs, various creepy-crawlies, birds. I tried to catch and expel rodents from the house; sometimes the cats got there first. Occasionally hummingbirds would dart in and could be persuaded to hop onto my finger for a ride back out the door.

I interfered, as part of the mountain's ecosystem. I spoiled a coyote's hunt one day. It was rare to see rabbits at our place. They are very secretive, unlike rabbits in Scotland. No surprise, considering the mountain's predators. I glanced out of the window and spied a rabbit lolloping below the garden, and thought: Unusual; how nice!

Just then (cue the menacing music) a coyote's head popped up from the lip of the slope not ten feet from the rabbit. I shrieked, threw the manuscript I was holding up in the air, and raced outside wildly waving my arms and wailing "My bunny! My bunny!"

It was not that I begrudged coyote his meal or put rabbits ahead of coyotes in my affections. It was just that I couldn't bear this particular moment of carnage, in my garden. I acted out of my nature, as coyote and rabbit act out of theirs. I didn't patrol the mountain, interfering with predators. Coyotes took one of my cats, in fact, when we were living in the tipi. We were part of the balances.

Coyote that day in the garden was peeved with me. He went around to my outhouse and howled. Coyotes are wary creatures but we saw them more often than we did rabbits. One night a coyote crossed the road in front of my truck. I stopped; the coyote paused on the edge of the forest, looking over his shoulder at me. Impulsively I called to him and he turned. I continued speaking to him. Remarkably, he came toward me. Up the bank onto the verge to stand watching me, almost near enough to touch. Suddenly I didn't know what to say. I became worried that another vehicle might come along. So I said thanks and goodbye, good luck, and hesitantly drove away.

Sometimes it is like that. Animals, all of us, act out of our natures, and those natures usually include curiosity and responsiveness. Coyote knew I didn't have a gun. Still, it is a chancy thing, approaching humans; I was grateful. Having wildlife flee from you is the flipside of having them attack, part of the species shuffle. Moments of trust or acceptance, extensions of interest, are to be cherished.

My friend Vlodya once had a yearling bear amble out of the forest and try to coax him into play, using motions like those of a frisky dog. Vlodya didn't dare play with him. For one thing, the bear was too big – would've hurt Vlodya even in fun. For another, like me with the roadside coyote, he worried that the bear might suffer fatal consequences if he came to regard humans as benign.

This is the saddest part of the story of humans and the rest of nature.

But not the thought I want to end on.

My neighbour Robin used to hike up to my place on Sundays during the winter to talk and practise guitar – my primary human contact during winters when I was alone. She brought Lilac, her happy-go-lucky dog with her one

Sunday, tying Lilac to a tree. My dog Leo was outside too, though not tied. When the two dogs got together they tended to go off and do bad-dog things.

It was a lovely Sunday, the snow fresh, knee-deep, the mountain immaculate. After our session in the house, Robin bundled up to walk home, went outside and found Lilac gone. Leo too. I bundled up, scunnered, and we began the search.

Living on the mountain involved a lot of outdoor physicality: cutting and hauling firewood, shovelling snow off the roof, maintaining two miles of access and the lines and drains for the gravity-feed water system, carrying supplies up the mountain, and so on. Even using the toilet entailed a short trek outdoors. Sometimes I'd lose the taste for walking the mountain just for pleasure.

The dogs' tracks were easily spotted but not easily followed. They went under the property line fence and through fir thickets on the adjoining National Forest land. The mountain, of course, is not level, and the dogs headed uphill. It looked like they were having a grand time. Joyful tracks. Looping and splitting off on separate canine tangents. Investigative; muzzle thrusts and furrows in the snow, dashes and flurried collaborations. Busy tracks. Here and thereness. Excitement. Deer sign, rabbit prints, a mouse's skitter.

We stumped and lunged along, whistling and calling for the dogs, to no avail. It was getting on in the day, starting to hint of an ink-blue twilight. We were

trudging under big ponderosa pines – trees that demand a lot of personal space; magnificent pines with their warm coppery bark, thick straight girths.

Robin and I still whistled and called, but at some point I had stopped feeling resentful at getting dragged away from my snug fireside to chase a couple of wayward dogs; and fell into a resonance, of place and companion, of sheer beauty.

We were still following the dogs' tracks, albeit in the dimness. But more than that, we were being led into the mountain's state of being. All pieces fitting together in relation to one another, a seamless whole. It is hard to describe without sounding corny, the picture of two friends on a winter mountain tracking two feckless dogs, moving more and more in tune with the vast power of life on that mountain. The snores of hibernating bears, sinuous sleep of reptiles, the hunters and hunted, deer drifting through the cedars, icy tinkle of creek, raven's croak echoing off the bluffs, frosty muzzle of coyote, lifted, sampling the scents on the cold currents of air.

The dog tracks took us in a long eccentric circle home, the dogs waiting for us there, guiltily pretending it was us who had taken a powder.

We pretended to chastise the dogs. It was the best walk we'd ever taken. Not electrifying like the first time I saw a cougar or heard a wolf, but a walk where each step was home.

SHE WAITS

In the evening the dog waits
for her boy to come home,
nose pointing down the long trail,
but darkness comes first
up the winter mountain.
She waits beneath a pine
then walks to the trail again
listening
tail drooping, waving a little,
hopeful, but no,
only a jay knocking cones
from the fir.
At full dark I whistle her in,
ruffle her ears: "He'll be home soon."
She waits inside the glass door
staring into the night, alert
for the crunch of boots in snow,
for his voice lightly hailing us
like the first star
in the evening's sky.

COMING HOME

Winter mountain night, its breath rimes the firs. Bears are dreaming in the mountain's pockets. Cubs gestate within their mothers as spring gestates within winter. I watch the moon move, stars move, between tree branches, the seated bulk of hills. Having harvested daylight and its revelations: ravens in the pale aspens; coyote running low as I laboured up the trail; two bald eagles black as ravens, white as snow, sailing on the afternoon quiet without a wing beat.

In winter I park the truck at the bottom of the mountain and walk home, a trek of several miles. My neighbour, Robin, does this also, her cabin a half-mile closer to our parking spot. We pull laundry, groceries and supplies on sleds or backpack them "like mules" as Robin said one day toiling under a bulky load. At first the driveway is a one-lane clay ribbon hugging the mountainside, rising, winding, dropping sheer on one side. It forks; our branch crosses 120 acres of field, cattail marsh, bluffs, hills and ridges with their steepled fir and pine, and the swift icy creek crowded by cedars, larch, yew and silver birch.

In winter the driveway narrows to a footpath trod by deer, coyotes, rabbits, grouse, mice and sometimes a fox or bobcat, as well as humans. Two shortcuts can reduce the distance home. The first is a high, steep hillside. Going down is often accomplished, like it or not, on your backside. Going up requires bracing and scrambling with hands as well as feet. Each time I opt for the shortcut I eye its uncompromising angle and height and affirm, "It is a good day to die." Once, climbing it with Gabriel, heavy-laden with packs, we'd just breathlessly hauled ourselves over the crest and collapsed for a rest when the gallon jug of milk Gabriel had set down sledded to the bottom of the hill. We watched open-mouthed its Olympic luge descent, and were stunned, caught between hilarity and weeping. Gabriel shed his pack and went to retrieve it.

On new moons, dark cold gathers under the trees. Walking home, using no flashlight, attention is concentrated in booted feet as they search out the path. The snow is faintly luminous, but under the trees darkness rules. The breath is loud; footsteps crunch; I waver, sometimes slip and stumble. Branches startle with sharp pokes or lightly whip my cheek as I pass, awkward, hurried, sweaty under the pack, cold in my extremities.

Then I pause and am enveloped in the mountain's slow breathing. The power

of place. It steadies me. I begin walking again, more quietly, more surely. My body remembers where the branches are, the dips, the outcrops. Somewhere a cougar stalks between straight towers of ponderosas; a grouse hunches in a snow cave and an owl hunts her.

The final winter before Gabriel went away to university, our vehicle broke down and there was no money for fixing it. Gabriel was teaching photography and doing office work thirty-five miles away – he had to find rides. He'd leave the house to descend the mountain before daybreak and later hike back up in the dark, usually bearing groceries, pet food, other supplies. We had no stocked reserves – a lean year. Mid-winter he got pneumonia, was wrackingly ill for eight weeks. Throughout, he continued his crepuscular treks up and down the mountain, to and from his work. He got very thin; his pack loads sometimes reached eighty pounds. There was no money for going to a doctor.

Illness lingered. Gabriel contrived a harness and travois for our dog, and she helped with hauling. He rebuilt our vehicle's carburettor, to no avail. "Are you ever afraid?" I asked Gabriel after his arrival home one night when shadows were so dense I could not imagine how he kept to the path. "There were a few times, early on," he admitted. "I saw dancing lights one night, and haven't felt afraid since." It is hard-earned, being at home with a mountain, being at peace with yourself.

Time is thought of as context, but it is not – relationship is, its dimensions and arrangements. Winter, the frozen lake, memories solid enough to walk on – crystallised. We study the patterns, the tracks in the snow. Mind skates on the surface of cold stillness, gradually losing momentum, slowing, listening. Beneath this stillness is a pulse, quiet as starlight, at this distance, solstitial. Starlight at proximity becomes sunlight, the eye of day, also solstitial.

These are our native rhythms, yet we live in denial or ignorance of the sources and ends of things; we institutionalise our own birthing and dying. To live in denial of cycles, consequences, natural processes, is to live in denial of relationship – context, memory – severed from awareness.

Where do the tracks in the snow lead? Who makes them? It is not linear: nothing on this curving earth, in this spiralling galaxy is linear. Where do we come from? Where do we go? *It is not linear.* Unmoving, the mountain constantly changes, life formed and transformed, an expressive vocabulary; can I be a foreign word here? My life is the land's; shortcuts not always a mercy.

HE CLIMBS

He climbs for the love
of high places.
Without counting his steps
he sings in his breath
as though the air
turns his heart
like a music box.

NAVIGATING

W e began in Pakistan, then crossed to Kashmir and like other visitors to Srinagar, stayed on a houseboat. A local man offered to guide us to Ladahk, taboo to westerners at that time. The guide had a jeep, and ponies for the latter part of the trek. I was sharply tempted, magnetised by the high country, mountains and settlements beyond western influence. But the guide seemed likely to rob and desert us, extort more money, or sell us to the authorities for defying travel restrictions. I said no. He disappeared as though conjured and dismissed by secret desires.

On some evenings in Srinagar we paddled a shikara on the lake among lotus lilies and ducks, mesmerised by the shimmy of reflected moonlight. A smooth-browed hill close to the lake, with a temple on its crown, rose against the sky. A winding walkway led to the temple and I joined the foot traffic of local devotees streaming up one morning. The temple was close-packed, a shuffling queue of chanting worshippers. A priest pressed ceremonial food into my hand, bending a quizzical glance at this stranger as I exited into the sunshine.

Looking down the hill from the temple, the eye encounters an inviting sweep of dried topaz grasses. I decided to take this direct route instead of the meditatively curving pathway. Contentedly swishing through the grasses, watching the lake come closer, I wondered why no one else chose this pleasant shortcut. Reaching the bottom of the hill I strolled past a knot of older men, one of whom reached a hand to delay me. "You know," he said gently, "there are probably more cobras on that hillside than anywhere else in Kashmir."

My capricious inner compass next pointed to India's heartland and the holy city of Benares (Varansi). Falling ill on the journey south, in Benares I drifted for days in a semi-conscious state brought on by food poisoning, dysentery and dehydration. Benares is considered a first-rate place in which to die – many pilgrims arriving for that very purpose, though that had not been my own plan. Still, it felt like a participatory tourism, lying in bed, deathly sick, listening to funeral chants and smelling the pyres' incense.

When my strength was sufficient we departed for Nepal and a healthier climate. From the mild Pokhara lowlands I raised my eyes to the legendary Himalayas – saw, on clear mornings, Annapurna, and felt powerfully on course. From higher Katmandu we took buses into the mountains. My companion despaired – I didn't even have destinations to name for him anymore. One afternoon we stepped off a bus in an isolated rural area, the only people to disembark. The sun was setting; already the thin warmth of day had fled. It was Himalayan November.

Shouldering packs, we trudged unspeaking past a few traditional dwellings, seeing no one. A short distance beyond the village we came on a deserted metal tower, like a fire look-out, its interior locked. We clanged up the metal stairs to the top where a railed balcony circled the core, and saw snow-covered mountains in every direction. The celestial kingdom. I was grateful for my companion's silence. This was not his idea; it was blustery and frigid and we had no food.

Putting on all the clothes from our packs, we scrunched into sleeping bags as darkness seized the land. I didn't sleep. All night the freezing wind raced between the mountains, over us, under us, spinning an icy web, singing in the metal gridwork. But the stars! No pollution, no electric lights; we were far above the mundane world. The stars blazed brilliant colours and like the wind, they sang. I listened all night, watching their journey. I looked down from them and saw myself small and dim but also singing, somewhere deep.

At dawn I stiffly shed the sleeping bag and stood at the railing. The clouds resting on the ridges parted, revealing the earth's highest peaks. Rose light illumined clouds and snow. The singing night, the mountain dawn: everything.

BAJA

———

Silence
lives in a cave
under wind
caught on cactus claw,
pivot of wingtip;
this is Coyote's realm,
tracks laid
over the silence,
the deep glittering dust,
the bones in the cave.

DESERTED

South of California is a long spine of Mexico called Baja, crowded on one side by the Sea of Cortez, on the other by the Pacific Ocean. Only the Sahara has more sunny days each year. We usually camped on the beach when visiting Baja, but sometimes were drawn to the interior deserts. Something about the interior seems so open yet so secretive that I'm never sure I'm actually seeing the desert when I'm in it.

It should be simple: cactus, lizard, cactus, snake, cactus, scorpion, cactus, cactus, buzzard, lizard, cactus, hawk, cactus, cactus…Endless arrangements of just a few life forms; or is it just a few? Deer, roadrunner, hummingbird, coyote, rabbit, lark, owl; gaze long enough and more and more inhabitants are discovered. How do they survive? The dry air shimmers with bird song. Where do they drink?

We walk. God it's hot. After a while alternatives cannot be imagined. The wind makes wave patterns on the sand. There are tracks of many careful creatures. The ground glitters, sweat stings my eyes, vanishes in the thirsty air. Cactus reaches out to snag me; I stop to pull thorns.

It is like an ocean – how are personal territories known here? It is sharp but never ending. The wind hums, navigating broad songlines. We trudge in a dry canyon of smooth white boulders. Sand squirts from the propelling feet of lizards detonated by our intrusion. We are seeking an oasis, have plodded some miles, eaten our desiccated sandwiches. The water bottles are almost empty – we should've brought more.

There is no moisture at the oasis. We blankly squint at the blowing sand. A dry year. It would be easy to die here. The oasis is mute; we turn back.

One night driving south, an on-coming car hits a large snake in front of us. It writhes, a scream-script of loops, then seems to snap its spine back into alignment. It glides off the road into the desert, a shaman snake.

Driving across the sands to volcanic mountains that for an hour look like they're ten minutes away. No trees or buildings for perspective, just rock and cactus and the hawks circling like toys with permanently crimped steering. Our car is a fragile habitat, the desert as perilous in its calm as a raging blizzard. A chilling calm – bones under a relentlessly cloudless sky.

We stop, venture out. The desert's mandala fascinate, one thing leading to another, yet pathless, and soon I am far from the car. A yellow snake flashes in front of me straight as a staff. How does it move like that?

At night the stars are sky cacti, prickles scattered in desert designs. Where we camp there are prints of coyote mother and pup criss-crossing the sands. In the middle of the night coyote mother comes to our tent and tries to drag away the heavy water jug. I hear the sound of it and stick my head out of the tent, coming face to face with her. She freezes, still gripping the jug.

"No, Coyote," I whisper to her. "We need our water." She drops it and evaporates into the cold Baja night. Next morning I finger her toothmarks on the plastic handle.

Where the desert meets the sea seems similar to where Baja meets California: the lean edge of survival meeting careless abundance. At neither border is there gradual transition; it's just one world, then the other. But each year the desert becomes less isolate. Plastic bags roll like tumbleweed and impale on cactus. Soiled toilet paper and disposable diapers, preserved in the dry air, speckle roadsides, oases, and camping accesses. The desert has not the drapery to hide pollution. Perhaps it will outlast it.

Time in the desert becomes both important and empty – action and patience, essential rhythm, non-linear chain reaction. It all seems so still, or at most surreptitious. Awareness needs to be unblinking. Even so you may miss most of what is there, despite all that light.

On one journey in Baja I celebrated New Year on the wrong day, somewhere losing twenty-four hours. I'm not sure if I dropped it all at once or if it dribbled out and evaporated an hour at a time while I walked across the sands.

Maybe coyote has it.

UNFINISHED SENTENCES

Evening, eastward clouds
backtracking the day;
clouds and walking, gestures
trailing the half-speech of yearning,
the life caught on grief's thorn.
Into the winter forest
each tree stilled in its
last thought of autumn;
hearing nothing but my footsteps
in this after-hours gallery.
Evening star poised above the hill
and trees waiting
like pilgrims at their destination.
I walk and sit
until the cold becomes a grace

CRUCIBLE

It was my husband's birthday. We had just finished hand-building a forty foot wooden barn for our goats and hay, and were living in a room at one end of it. Our belongings were stored in the hayloft along with family antiques of my mother's. Our one-room household encompassed baby's crib, our bed, a plank table, cooking stove and heating stove. Also three cats. There was a knothole in the wall separating our room from the goats. As soon as we stirred in the mornings, a representative goat would press her nose to the knothole and BAAA! at us, the other goats chorusing in the background.

Our cedar-kindled fire escaped the stovepipe that birthday morning in April, and immediately flared out of control, licking across the wood ceiling. We had no water. I pulled on trousers and shirt (intuitively grabbing my best) and ran outside carrying two-year old Gabriel. I drove the truck down the hill and locked him in, racing barefoot back up the hill into the burning barn to call the fire department.

The call was answered by a fussy woman who repeatedly requested I spell my husband's last name and explain why on earth I was telephoning the fire department. With flames careering overhead, I felt as though trapped in the nightmare where your house is burning around you and a voice on the telephone conversationally keeps asking you to spell your husband's name.

I dropped the phone, running to help my husband – he of the birthday and the long last name – to bring our goats to safety. A maddened Hercules, I ripped fence-posts from winter-hard ground and hauled squalling goat mamas and babies from their stalls. Chaos. Babies darted back into the burning barn in search of mamas and frantic mamas tore loose from our grasps to chase after babies. My mother's chickens exited on their own; the cats were nowhere to be seen. The big male goat was rescued last, fainting in an odoriferous heap from all the excitement, having to be dragged out prone, the pride of the herd.

The barn was an inferno. I sprinted to my mother's cabin: shouted at her to bring water – a futile gesture. Running back, close to attaining the buck's swoon into oblivion, I saw my husband duck into the fire and emerge shoving our rototiller. Gasoline exploded; I screamed at him to run. The building was a hell, rolling black smoke and roaring flames. I could hear my stash of home-canned goods detonating in the loft.

The fire department arrived in time to save the surrounding forest and fields; the building burned to the ground. Nothing salvaged but the goats, chickens and ourselves. We had no insurance and no money. The loss stunned the mind, but more searing was the betrayal of heart. One of the cats turned up several days after the fire and for several more days circled the scorched site, crying.

I sifted obsessively through deep, stinking ashes. They smouldered for days – hundreds of hay bales had been consumed. Miraculously I found my mother's family jewellery, but even the diamonds were ruined. I pulled out remnants of tools: shovel blades, pitchfork tines, twisted, melted objects recognised only after much perplexity, and made a heap of things that were still things. All of it worthless, but I couldn't let it all go at once. Lastly I found the remains of one cat, her grotesquely charred body no longer resembling anything but the grievousness of loss.

Sixteen years later, in the mountains, in the eighth year of drought, the forests conflagrated. Day by day, temperatures sweltered in the high nineties, sometimes higher. The sun kept us under house arrest, slowly glaring past, curling the edges of the tomato leaves, turning the soil to ash-like dust. I watered the garden twice a day, like a kindly guard in a prison camp, the eye of the sun unblinking.

Forest fire is part of living in the American west, but that summer was notable. A tossed cigarette started one, lightning ignited others. Hundreds of thousands of acres burned. Birds fled like smoke from torched trees; ragged animals haunted the outskirts of towns, homeless, driven from their ranges. Day after day, no rain. Thunder muttered in the hills, no friendly sound. Lightning lashed hilltops, a game of pyrotechnics using whole trees as tinder – volatile conifers exploding into fireballs. Some lightning storms left hundreds of new blazes in their wakes.

The west became a war zone. Firefighters from distant states converged, living in tent cities, in football fields, communities within communities. An all-woman team of Navajo fire-fighters arrived from New Mexico. Small aeroplanes droned through the shimmering, heated air, dropping fire retardant. Helicopters racketed over rivers and lakes, lowering metal containers into the water, the buckets dangling like ponderous sacrifices below the insect shapes of the choppers.

Daily reports were posted at the laundromat: what areas should be evacuated; where new fires had erupted; how containment was going; what the weather was predicted to be. No panic, just endurance, and the fatalism peculiar to the west. People live with daily reminders that the elements are not domesticated. It is still a big outdoors. Firefighters in Colorado died that summer. Helicopters beat the air and thunder woke us in the stifling suspense of night, and still it didn't rain.

Wind's furnace blew, foiling attempts to curb the fires' spread. Isolated blazes converged, one day reaching the ridge overlooking the town two miles from where I lived. Scant yards into its descent toward us the flames were turned back by a fickle shift of wind. We took a collective breath, returned to doing laundry, posting letters, errands and tasks that go on until the end.

My neighbour drove up to my place with a message one night. A friend had spotted flames in a roadless area of the forest. My neighbour and I lived without electricity or phones, isolated. "What are you going to do?" she asked. It was about nine o'clock at night. I considered for some minutes. "Go to bed. What about you?" She laughed, shrugged. "Me too." But Gabriel put the CB in our truck where it could be plugged into the cigarette lighter, and I stood for a long time at the window, scanning the mountainside, trying not to flinch at each lightning flash, praying.

I prayed many times that summer as fires raged. There were days when the choking sting of smoke in the air became so heavy I closed the windows, trying to seal it out. One day I was in the garden watering the bravely abiding vegetables. Smoke shrouded the sun, casting a sullen, sickly glow melding with the dull radiance of fires on the western horizon. There was a feeling of apocalypse, of diminishing sluggish struggle beneath the oppression of heat and uncertainty.

I prayed aloud as I watered; prayed for the land, the animals, the people. My voice sounded small, without resonance. It stopped mid-sentence, silenced as though words had turned to ash, weightless against the pressure of that shrouded light. I stood rooted, lips still parted, surrounded by rooted trees, all of us waiting, alive, flammable.

PART THREE ANIMAL TALES

JANUARY DAWN

January dawn –
a rocky quarter-mile of shore,
three hunched herons.

FINDING THE DOOR

February afternoon at Tormore, on Skye. Sitting beside the cottage, a creature walked past me. First impression: a stoat on steroids. No, bigger than that. An otter. He was walking, back humped, along the fence and retaining wall that line the driveway.

I dashed into the cottage for my camera, dashed back out; the otter was continuing along the top of the wall, toward the road. Every few yards he stopped to peer down, hopeful, but the wall was too high and sheer for descent. I followed at a distance – the otter hadn't yet noticed me. My plan was to slowly overtake the otter, dissuading him from reaching the danger of the road. He'd already been in trouble of some kind – walked with one back paw tucked up under his tummy, and had a wound in the groin, a scrape by his whiskery mouth.

Near the end of the driveway the otter disappeared. The embankment sloped down to the base of the wall where a ditch held water. As expected, the otter paused there; I could hear him rustling and squelching in the narrow ditch. When I peeked over the wall the otter was about four feet away from me. He looked up, froze. Distress was explicit in his stare, the lowered serpentine neck and head, bared teeth, flattened stance; he started growling and mewling. It was at once intimidating and heartbreaking.

I snapped photos, feeling like a brute, justifying it with the necessity to keep him from the road. He muddled in place, then turned back, retracing his trek along the drive, again pausing every few yards to crane his neck over the wall, looking for a way down. Again I followed at a distance, thinking to herd him toward the sea.

He found the break in the wall, emerged on the driveway, and crossed to the cottage. I could've kicked myself for not having left the cottage door or the door of the walled garden open. The injured otter could then have been confined, giving me a chance to phone Skye's otter rescue centre. Those route possibilities shut, the otter – noting my approach – skirted the cottage and slipped through the gate bars of the walled sheep park.

There are only two openings to the park: the gate by the cottage, where I now stood, and the gate leading into the fank. I watched the otter steadily limp along the base of the wall. The sheep spooked, scattering across the park. At the first corner, the otter turned and continued along the perimeter, turned again at the next corner, and systematically started up the third side of the square. I reckoned he'd escape through the fank gate, cross the fank and slip out the other side onto the moor. Tormore is on the shore – he wouldn't have far to go to get back to the water.

It was not to be that simple. Several tups stood between the otter and the gate. As the otter neared, the tups explosively snorted and stamped their feet. The scattered sheep instantly mobilised, rushing to the tups. I'd never before witnessed such solidarity. The sheep stood at attention, bunched in front of the gate, staring at the otter.

The otter stopped. Stared at the sheep. Then lowered himself to the ground and rolled onto his back, paws in the air.

He stayed that way for a few minutes, occasionally rolling onto his side. The sheep gradually relaxed, started grazing. The otter rose, then, and walked away from them, cutting diagonally across the park to the wall nearest the shore. He located the lowest portion of wall, scaled it, snaked down the other side, and threaded his way among the rocks to the water's edge.

The sea appeared absolutely still, glassy, blurring into the colourless sky, no horizon line. The otter slid into the water with hardly a ripple, gliding out of sight around the skerry like a silent arrow drawn by an invisible string, into dimensionless grey. Leaving me in the world.

SMALL SOUNDS

Tick of the stovepipe,

tap of madrone berries,

talk of the birds

as they feed in the fog.

Do they listen

to my small sounds?

Scratch of writing,

floorboard's creak,

soft fall of herbs into bowls.

The cat watches my listening,

reflects it

as one leaf, another,

lets go

RELATIONS

Every evening our cat Topaz leaped to a windowsill in the living room to watch for a handsome fox who appeared to be courting her. Topaz was fluffy and orange with a gorgeous plumed tail – a neutered female. The fox serenaded Topaz with what seemed to me unmelodic vocalisations beneath the window. Topaz preened but showed no inclination to go outside during the fox's visits. A wise feline wariness: courtship is one thing, a snuff scene another.

While washing dishes one afternoon I heard a ruckus and saw my male cat Taj hotly pursued by the fox. I dashed out as cat and fox careened around the corner of the house, streaking toward me. Both were going flat-out, pedal to the metal. Taj flashed up the porch steps between my feet and crouched there, panting. The fox, intent, didn't slow, so I shouted "Stop! You can't have my cat!"

The fox stopped, almost at my feet. A stand-off. Cat vibes running up my leg said, "Yeah, momma, you tell him!" The fox stiffly backed, pivoted and trotted away. He paused to glance over his shoulder – I could've sworn he smiled – then bounded off. Relieved cat vibes billowed. We went inside. Topaz, at her window seat, looked disappointed at her suitor's departure. We never saw him again at the house.

It was not the last of the fox's presence, however. A broad weedy hill – an old hay field – rose from the side of the farmyard. I would sense the fox's attention. Sighting of him would not be immediate. An emptying of intentional search, then I'd spot him sitting on the hillside amid the grasses. He was always facing me – seemed to know when my gaze located him. A telescoping of distance, gazes locked. Then the fox would stand, glide away into the weeds; or I would turn away, freeing him.

Each in our own terms, the relationship went beyond mere surveillance. I felt a mutuality. For all his bright pelt, the fox is a secretive creature. I was sympathetic to that far-off yet intense regard, that alert patience as he studied the situation. Whatever the fox concluded from this scrutiny, I appreciated that it was more than cursory. Like Topaz, I was disappointed when the fox finally seemed to disappear for good. The hill became like an empty house.

The fox was not the only wild creature to stare through the window that year. I was working at my desk one winter afternoon when the certainty of being

watched drew my attention outside. A snowy owl, something not usually seen in that part of the country, was seated on the fence-post in the yard, indeed staring. Her head would uncannily swivel away, then turn back to gaze at me with mad-looking yellow eyes. Owls, even more than foxes, seem to belong to themselves, and this ghostly owl with her unearthly beauty seemed quite inscrutable. Our mutual staring did not so much open mutual understanding as seemed a venture into alien perspective. A few days after this, the owl returned and dropped an immaculate dead ermine by the porch.

The ermine was unmarked except for lethal but tidy talon punctures in his neck. A pouch was made from this enigmatic gift. When I stroked the silky fur I mused: white owl, white human, white ermine, white snow. The resonance remained. Like the fox the owl did not return, but time never weakened the visitation of those gazes.

RAVEN KNOWLEDGE

Who will lose;

How to summon wolves;

Who will be next;

How to warn others;

Who has crossed the boundary;

What will happen,

What will happen.

NATURE'S NATURE

I got a call from a stranger asking, "Is this the bird lady?" He brought over a crow in a cardboard box; one wing had been shattered on a power-line. I took the bird to the vet, who said the wing would have to be amputated, which he wouldn't do unless I agreed to adopt the bird. The crow survived the operation and came home with me, living first in our screened-in porch, then in a larger wire enclosure we attached to the house. I called the crow Asaroka, or Roka, and made perches for him in the enclosure. His sleeping perch was under the house eaves to give shelter from stormy weather.

I visited Roka several times a day. Gradually he accepted my presence and perched on my hand to take food, but became alarmed at anyone else entering his space. Flightlessness made him vulnerable, nervous and depressed. He was not a happy bird. Roka never spoke after a first wild "CAW!" when he woke from the anaesthesia to discover he no longer could fly. When other crows passed by the house he hunched, silent, not wanting to be seen. My company was no comfort to him.

Physically, except for the missing wing, he was healthy. His feathers shone and he jumped vigorously (obsessively) from perch to perch all day. He ate well; he preened his feathers and splashed mightily in the bath pan. When the wind blew, which it often does with great force on the Olympic Peninsula where we lived, Roka would turn to face it, lifting his wing and lowering his head. His eyes gleamed. The wind rushed through his feathers. Crows often play in the wind, doing acrobatics. Wind and bird are partners. Roka was not a baby bird – he remembered flight, its freedom and pleasure.

Roka escaped once. He lunged from branch to branch on an evergreen near the house until he was perched at the tip top. He would not come down. Plainly happy there – ecstatic-looking, in fact – he ruffled and preened his feathers over and over. He stretched his neck and excitedly peered around.

I let him be for several hours. At dusk I made the decision to bring him back inside. My husband shook the tree until Roka fluttered to a smaller tree where I caught him. The bird was upset; I wept. If I had to do it again, I think I would let him go his way, to be free. I didn't want him to starve or be killed – to suffer – but he suffered anyway.

Roka was with us for less than a year. One night a fat racoon tunnelled under the wire and took him away. Roka never made a sound. Two feathers were all I found. The abduction didn't seem natural. The night it happened I woke in a cold sweat from a nightmare of intrusion. My husband, usually a profound sleeper (he once slept through an earthquake) woke also, uncharacteristically afraid, saying he thought someone was in the house. He went downstairs, baseball bat in hand, but found no one. Next morning we realised Roka had been taken by the racoon.

I still think about Roka, the one-winged crow who knew he should be able to fly. I remember a childhood of jumping off roofs and falling hard. When I see crows now, I feel I know something about them. I know how their feathers feel and are arranged. I know the feel of their feet as they perch, their weight, and the sharpness and texture of their beaks. I know the motions they make while swallowing food and their manner of intently peering at objects. Their paranoia and mischief are familiar and so is their intelligence and sensitivity. When I think of Roka I like to picture him as a nestling come again to this life with two strong wings, launching into his first flight in the morning sun. Winds take him high.

WINTERKILL

No blame –
it just happens;
I hear coyotes exulting
over their discovery
and in the morning
the dog starts
bringing home bones
one by one
like the days
until spring.

NEIGHBOURS

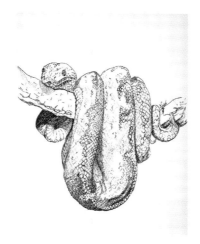

When my neighbour and I bought our place on the mountain, the realtor cannily informed us that we weren't being charged any extra for the rattlesnakes, which is good because there are a fair number of them. We tried to maintain cordial relations with the reptiles despite their lack of market value.

Cindy, a neighbour down the mountain, tried to do the same, though there was one rattler her husband shot when it came into their tent and wouldn't leave. It had fourteen rattles, so must've been prodigious. Two of the snakes that visited our dwelling were humongous and many-rattled too. Maybe some kind of middle-aged ennui compels rattlesnakes of a certain maturity to slide in search of adventure among humans.

I went to town for plumbing fixtures one day, making a pile of CPVC elbows and connectors that, during my wait for the counterman's attention, I arranged into fanciful configurations. When he finally finished discussing the mysteries of submersible pumps with the customer ahead of me, the salesman remarked that my plumbing design looked like a snake, which unleashed his recollections of rattlesnake encounters. Each tale concluded with the Slewing of the Reptile by various means – of dispatch, not combat. I nodded and ummed throughout. The salesman wanted more, though; his look became pleading. "You just leave them alone, don't you!" he abruptly accused.

Were we about to embark on a meaningful conversation there in the plumbing store? I opened my mouth but a second salesman cut in, pronouncing with a finality that silenced the entire store: "I kill ever' one of 'em I kin find."

Well! Here was a man who would know how to deal with a recalcitrant faucet.

Over the nearby Canadian border, I could recklessly stride through tall grass, knowing the area to be rattlesnake-free. But at home I had to tread carefully. Especially at the store.

On the mountain we became masters of the Close Call. Our dog almost trampled over a rattler once, unaware of the snake. It reared and struck at her, fangs just brushing her. She trembled for a good while after. How did she know it for something poisonous, life-threatening? Silly questions, once you've seen one of these muscle-bound monsters.

Another time, a visiting friend of my son's was tramping down the hill in the dark on a cold autumn night, heading for our car. His knee was lightly struck by what he thought was a stick. When he realised it was a rattler the horrified youth rocketed onto the top of the car and crawled in through the window. He trembled for a good while too. Snakes often heat-seek under recently active vehicles. Our young friend was lucky that the rattler was still too sluggish with cold to make an effective strike.

On a much warmer occasion – one, in fact, where I'd left the house doors open for ventilation, and our cat Biskie was dozing in one doorway – I looked up from a conversation with Vlodya to see a rattler gliding into view, inches from the cat. The usual cardiac reaction to seeing a rattlesnake was compounded by the fact of open door and proximity to beloved pet.

Biskie froze, squinched shut her eyes in denial. It was a lo—ng snake, a slow, liquid glide. I crouched, not wanting to startle the cat into the snake's path. "Here Biskie, here kitty." This, in the tiniest of quavering voices. "Here Biskie, Biskie."

The cat bolted. Toward me. Massive relief, sweat swiped from forehead with trembling forearm.

I cuddled the cat; Vlodya went cautiously outside to follow the snake. The image burned into my mind is of looking at the wide doorway and seeing that viperous head appear, then the body, then more body, more body, still more body to come after the head had disappeared from the frame. Endless snake. And poor Biskie. She never again lay in that doorway. In fact, she took to snoozing above the kitchen cupboards: high ground. Though it was only the first of two rattlesnake encounters for her.

We developed a system for moving rattlesnakes (which are territorial, as are we) when discovering them close to the house. A designated metal garbage bin would be laid on its side and the snake encouraged to enter it – sometimes by lifting the snake with a (long) piece of steel rebar – the rebar then used to upright the bin. On with the metal bin cover, secured with bungee cords, and into the car with the bin.

We would drive the snake to a particularly out of the way part of our land (no, not down to the neighbours) that was suitable rattlesnake habitat, and reverse the capture procedure. During the car ride the snake, understandably irate, would ferociously rattle, a terrifying sound made worse by the metal bin's amplifying properties. All you could do was pray to the god of bungee cords.

The rattling these snakes provide as a warning is an inexplicable kindness, as the snakes are so naturally camouflaged that you rarely see them until you are literally upon them. It is a chilling sound, sets your hair on end, and I admired Gabriel's calm one day when he called to me that he'd just kicked a big rattlesnake.

"Is it rattling?" I asked, across the field.

"Yes," he said, "What should I do?"

"Apologise!"

Which he appeared to be doing.

"Is it still rattling?"

"No," he said, making safe retreat. You want to stay on peaceful terms with neighbours like these.

There's a fine cave on our land, up in the cliffs, where we're told the rattlesnakes like to pile together to hibernate. Local men used to scramble up there to kill the snakes. When we moved onto the mountain a group of these men came up and asked if they could go do one of their annual massacres. They were told, diplomatically but frankly, that we didn't want to get the snakes riled up; that we'd just as soon live and let live with whatever made its home on the mountain.

The men allowed that this was not beyond their understanding. They shuffled their feet, seemed reluctant to leave. "Can we go up and just *look* at 'em?"

This was OK. Robin went with them. The cave was empty, but it didn't seem to matter. It was another of those occasions when it becomes apparent that people – including loggers and ranchers – have a craving to just be out on the land, maybe see some wondrous thing. Killing is just the masculine excuse.

Except, of course, for the man of mission at the plumbing store.

WHAT BIRDS LISTEN TO

This is what birds

listen to –

muffled static of wind,

whitenoise:

the message from space never comes.

GETTING THE MESSAGE

Being on my own so much, I took to talking with Leo, our dog. I talked to the cats too, but they tended to squint and let it all roll past unless I mentioned food. Leo was more sympathetic. Like one of those "non-directive" psychologists. She'd reflect my feelings back to me, consolingly. I always felt better after confiding in Leo.

Most of my communications with wildlife involved body language and "vibe" rather than words, which was instructive. For instance, learning not to smile at birds or animals who don't appreciate a show of teeth; likewise not to point, gun-like. Other times my communications were merely imitative – trying to copy animal vocalisations. The only ones I was even slightly good at were coyotes and crows or ravens. (My sister can do owl calls, learned during her work for the Forest Service.) I could divert crows from their flight paths; they'd circle around looking for the (fake) crow.

But my imitations were not so much communication as self-indulgence. It was exciting to set off the coyotes, like setting off a series of signal fires: the howling of one (me) would trigger howling all along the ridge or valley. Once, Gabriel came out of the tipi in a boisterous mood and let rip a fine yodel, cacophonously answered by a slew of coyotes so close by that Gabriel's hair stood on end. Coyotes can't resist the challenge of a howl. Wait 'til they hear bagpipes!

I took my frame drum outside on a sunny morning to an outcrop overlooking a clearing. As I pattered away on the drum, a male turkey suddenly strode into the clearing as if onto a stage. Turkeys being prey to coyotes, cougars, and the like, usually are quite reticent. But this turkey strutted and boogied back and forth in full view, in time to the drum.

I tried variations, tapped the rim of the drum; the turkey responded, gobbling excitedly, doing a kind of Michael Jackson routine. I expected him to take a bow when I stopped, but he just boogied away into the forest.

Similar, perhaps, was a male grouse who "displayed" at me one time. He dashed out into the driveway where I was walking, and like a small flasher did his avian "come hither" thing. I tried to express proper admiration without committing myself. The grouse repeated his display several times – stretched tall, fluffed up, tail spread, doing a wee dance. Then dashed away.

Obviously, with these bird encounters the communication was unsought and mutually garbled, though a naturalist or professional wildlife communicator could've interpreted. I attempted to convey a deliberate message to some ants, once, when I was living in Michigan. Carpenter ants infiltrated some of my roof rafters – damp wood. I could see the ants marching in at the eaves, actually hear them munching the wood. Big ants.

I ran a couple hundred feet of electrical extension cord from my mother's cabin to ours, and plugged in her hoover. Set a ladder against the wall, climbed up with the hoover, and began vacuuming ants. Panic ensued, but I got a fair number sucked up before the rest hid behind the wall boards. I liberated the ants out of the hoover bag outside.

This process was repeated several times, but ants are not fools. It got so that as soon as I *touched* the hoover the ants would panic and hide. Then, all it took was me *thinking* about the hoover and they'd become highly agitated and hide.

This was interesting. Also discouraging, as I no longer could get near the ants with the hoover. Since they seemed sensitive to my intentions, I decided to try sending them a mental message.

I formulated a horrendous doomsday-for-ants image in my mind. An explicit holocaust. And projected this, visualising ants fleeing my house as their only salvation.

Next day the ants were gone. Every last one.

Coincidence? Mebbe. But it was cool.

Mostly I went in for receptive rather than projective communication with wildlife. I used to dream about whales: one dream was of being able to hear and translate whale songs by sticking my hand into the sea. This may have to do with feeling that in order to understand something you need to enter its native arena, or at least venture to bridge the realms.

My husband and I took our canoe to Baja to see the whales, in the lagoon where they calve. Watching whales from a boat, even an open canoe, isn't the same as being in the water with them, but is a step in that direction. We felt vulnerable indeed in that fragile boat, watching grey whales explode from the sea and crash back again in glittering curtains of spray – recalling the kayaker who got pancaked by a whale's tail when he came too close.

We kept an ample distance away, content to be able to glimpse the whales poking heads or tails out of the water, leaping, the mist of their exhalations hanging in the air, the sound of their breathing carrying across the water. Sitting quietly in the canoe communicated interest; making no attempt to approach communicated respect. At least we hoped so.

I don't like chasing close encounters with wildlife. Better when they happen naturally in the course of daily life. When you are receptive and paying attention, they do happen. If you sit still long enough or move unobtrusively enough. If you are in the right place at the right time.

Rob and I were hiking at the north end of Trotternish, on Skye, heading for Rubha Hunish. At Duntulm Rob pointed out a fabulous creature in the water; it looked unreal, something dreamed up in a movie studio. I was incredulous. "Basking shark," Rob told me, having seen many of them in Loch Fyne when he was a kid.

We continued to Rubha Hunish where we wandered below magnificent cliffs, clambered along the shore admiring sea stacks, poked around tidal pools; a beautiful day, a beautiful place. I sat above the shore before leaving and spontaneously made a prayer of thanks, tossing a traditional American Indian offering into the sea.

A whale rose to the surface so close I jumped to my feet, galvanised. As it slid past another whale rose, then a third. I was beside myself with excitement and pleasure. Whales! These encounters are part of an ongoing conversation with the universe.

LOCAL

Flattened compost bin –
the rummaging bear sat on it,
went on
burly among the firs.

Cougar surging up the bluffs –
glimpsed from upstairs –
tawny jolt
while tightening the bedspread's corners.

Lifting boards from the lumber pile –
rattler
coiled, flawless,
my breath fled.

BIG

When I was buying milk at the general store one day I glanced out the window as the school bus trundled by. I glimpsed the driver, a middle-aged local man, and saw him as if in two worlds at once – this one and 'elsewhere'. It raised the hair on me. I pulled myself together and paid for the milk. A week later the driver was shot dead while dropping off a child during the regular bus run.

These moments now and then occur; strange lurches of reality. What do they add up to? Who knows. Mystery's big footprint. Mystery being big doesn't make the ordinary small. The ordinary is intricate – many footprints – astonishing. I think of the big ordinary on the mountain; I think of …bears.

Our first bear sighting on the mountain happened when my land partner Robin was down by the creek building a temporary lodge in which to do a sweat, right after we moved onto the land. The bear came ambling up the old logging trail by the creek. No one had lived on the land for as long as locals could recall, so the bear was not on the alert for human encounter. The bear didn't seem on the alert for anything, actually, even given the poor vision of ursines in general.

Robin stood beside her wee lodge, wearing a red vinyl raincoat, waiting for the bear to notice her.

Dum-de-dum; the bear ambled closer, closer, closer. Then – ACH! – saw Robin when he nearly trod on her.

He ran away.

Most bears we encountered ran away from us. Still, there is something about being in bear country – coming upon warm piles of bear shit, or stumps newly ripped open; or seeing the bears themselves, that excites every nerve.

When Gabriel and I were living in a tipi, we felt the vulnerability of an unequipped species. The notion of "good relations" left the comfort of the conceptual and spread with haste through our bodies. Harmony was something to feel fervent about. We wanted to cultivate this medicine.

Part of our tipi's interior – the west part, as is traditional – was reserved as a place of honouring. For guests and for our medicine. A road-killed great horned owl (minus meaty parts) hung with outspread wings in the west. Above the doorway, in the east, likewise hung a rough-legged hawk. Our dog Leo helped

look after the tipi in a more conventional manner. Leo is fairly big – mostly shepherd, maybe some husky mixed in; big in size and big in mission. She once tried to defend us from a gargantuan rattlesnake bent on getting into the tipi. Pacific rattlers are notoriously aggressive. They scare Leo, but she has mission, and this is especially evident when it comes to bears.

One day when Gabriel and I – and Leo – were away, a bear decided: Aha! good time to raid the tipi. When we got home there was the door-flap fecklessly torn from the tipi, cast into the bushes. A large, perfect, muddy bear print on the door-flap confirmed identification of our visitor. Dismayed, we peeked into the tipi, expecting chaos, wreckage, destruction.

There was mud just inside the doorway. A few hawk feathers lay on the ground. The tipi's interior was absolutely undisturbed.

We stared across the tipi at the great horned owl in full predatory flight, then at the hawk talons dangling so they brush your head when you duck through the door opening. We looked at each other and smiled, picturing the bear flinging aside the door-flap and barging in to be confronted by the sight of the owl and the rake of hawk talons through his fur, looking up in panic to see that hawk looming right overhead.

Way to go, birds.

We immortalised the print by replacing mud with paint, and refastened the door-flap to the tipi. Bear medicine joined bird medicine. The tipi was looking good.

The next bear visit came after we moved into the house, but hadn't yet installed doors. The bear just walked in at about six o'clock one morning. I was asleep upstairs; Leo was asleep downstairs. She woke when the bear entered; I was wakened by simultaneously surprised bear and surprised dog sounds.

The bear rushed out the door. The dog gave chase. I charged (naked) downstairs shouting for Leo to come back, trailing a poor third behind bear and dog.

Even after these unsuccessful forays, bears continued to visit now and then, usually to topple our compost pile. When Gabriel got a snazzy store-bought compost bin, a bear came by, tipped it over, then sat on it, completely flattening it, which seemed uncalled for. The other bear-play we endured regularly was their biting through our PVC waterline. Perhaps they enjoyed the drinking-fountain effect.

I was sitting in the living room, staring out the glass doors, Leo asleep on the rug, when another visit occurred. I say I was staring out the doors but really I was staring at my thoughts, because for a good while I didn't notice the bear.

Our two cats noticed right off. They fluffed up in giant hedgehog mode and jumped to a windowsill, peering in outrage at the bear. This behaviour finally penetrated my reverie. Why were the cats acting so funny? Then I noticed that there was a large animal muzzle showing at the bottom-right of the glass doors where I'd earlier set out corncobs for the cats to gnaw.

"Only Leo," my mind reasoned. But Leo was asleep at my feet. The bear moved fully into view, inches from the glass.

"It's a bear!" (exclaimed aloud).

"No shit!" sneered the look both cats burned over their shoulders at me.

Recently there was a bear who visited while my mother was staying alone at our place. My mother is used to wildlife coming and going from her house in Michigan. She leaves doors open. We'd instructed her not to leave *our* doors open, however, because having a rattlesnake in the closet is not like having a garter snake nestled there. But Barbara went for a walk, left the cat, Jumpers, in the house and the door open. When she came back the half-glass of milk she'd left on the counter was on the floor, an apple was missing from the fruit-bowl, and Jumpers was acting cuddly – which translates into traumatised.

She figured Jumpers had knocked the milk glass over. The missing apple was a puzzle until she noticed fierce gouges on the upright piano, and books and tapes that had been on top of the piano now scattered on the floor.

Poor kitty! Clearly, a bear had been in, given attention to his snack, then to Jumpers, who must've leaped onto the piano looking for high ground away from swiping bear paws. Later, my mother discovered that a plastic five-gallon bucket of food she'd set in the creek-bed to cool, was gone, leaving the image of a happy bear lolloping along through the woods with his very own lunch-pail.

Having scored so well, this bear returned. Gabriel photographed him outside the house – a yearling, probably, by his size. He went inside Robin's cabin too. On one occasion, Robin's teenage daughter was napping upstairs, woke and came down to find the bear rummaging through the fridge. Cupboards already pillaged. On another occasion Robin and Gia came home to find that the bear had eaten all their grapes, leaving clean-picked stems in a neat pile on the floor.

On the subject of neat piles, my mother and I took a walk, with Jumpers, along the base of the cliffs that rise on the upper boundary of our land. Jumpers likes to go for walks, racing ahead, zipping up and down trees, then lagging behind and complaining when he gets tired, but refusing to be carried. During a pause in this walk he suddenly went into GHM (giant hedgehog mode) as he sniffed around where we stood.

He'd found a very big, neat pile of cougar shit, lightly covered with dirt. The cougar's "sunburst etching", scraped around the mound, was impressive. Jumpers hastily dug a shallow cup right beside the cougar mound and hunched over it (still in GHM) to bravely create a wee mound of his own.

When I moved to the Isle of Skye, in Scotland, I found a similar bigness of elemental land (and sea) scape: and outrageous weather – aye big. But in a place now bereft of large land animals other than livestock and deer, and where indigenous humans have been chivvied aside in favour of sheep and southern incomers, big has had to endure in dispersion, in dialect, in roots and crags and unremarked continuities. A yew tree 5,000 years old grows, still, in a churchyard in Perthshire, across the road from a neolithic stone circle. Lewisian gneiss, 3,000 million years old, steadies the Hebrides. Not a flash-in-the-pan place.

Standing on the shore where we live, I hear the breathing of dolphins as they pass, the alternating thrill and suspense as they surface and dive, scarcely troubling the waters. I see porpoises, seals, otters. Herons pose, gulls wheel like gnats; one day a peregrine alighted on the garden path – the sight catching me at the kitchen sink when I raised eyes used to resident blackbirds and finches and instead saw this sleek falcon parked beneath the rose bush. Like seeing a Formula One parked at the church, or Pele on a hopscotch board.

Living in a big landscape keeps human things in perspective. With that comes pleasure in both the immense surprise of the ordinary, and the everyday presence of mystery, not in the abstract, but in immediate reality. Like the heart-stopping sight of a whale rising beside your boat; in the unprogrammed instant, you realise: big.

WHAT IS CARRIED

In the medicine bag:
one of my son's baby teeth

and a tuft of black-cat fur and

a stone I've had so long
memory has been smoothed away, sealed
in sunsets, sunrises,
every rounded stillness;

coyote fur;

the shard of baby whalebone from
an isle off Baja and

the broken gold crown from
dental work my father paid for
that suicidal year;

smokey quartz from
an earring my mother gave me;

two other stones (Callanais?)
I should remember

and a slender tooth and claw from
the wildcat who chewed two legs off
getting free of a trap,
dying in my frost-killed garden,
buried there.

NOVEMBER

Vlodya and I were in the cosy living room, reading in the failing afternoon light when – BAM! – a furry body flung itself against the picture window beside us. An intense golden-eyed face stared up at me. A bobcat.

She withdrew; I darted to another window for vantage. The bobcat peered at me from around the edge of a straw bale near the house. Those lighted eyes, ears with their high tufted tips. She drew back again and I eased outside, catching sight of her at the base of the terraced garden. She turned once more to look at me, then vanished over the lip of the hillside.

I didn't know what to make of it. Bobcats are perhaps the most reticent of all the mountain's denizens. In a decade I'd only seen their tracks, never a glimpse of the wildcats who made them. Why would she approach the house at all – especially with the dog present – much less throw herself against the window?

That night passed, and the next day. Night came again. It was cold, the ground stark, patchy with snow. I looked out the window and saw her lying on her side in the garden, dead. Shocked, I went to her, knelt and stroked her. The fur soft and thick, shaded and marked with russet, grey, black, cream. I was confronted with what excitement blinded me to the day she first came – both paws on her right side were gone. Chewed off, no doubt by herself. The front paw at the first leg joint, the other higher up. Both stumps were scabbed over – she'd chewed the paws off days before her death. How could I not have seen?

I lifted her body – feather-light. She had died of starvation. Despite her reclusive nature, her suffering in a manmade leghold trap; despite the presence of the dog, she had come to my house for help. I would've been so glad to give it.

We buried her in the garden, with a little offering of milk. I searched for a long time but couldn't find the leghold trap. I did find the trapper's bootprints in the snow. But the image of the bobcat is the mark that does not fade.

SPRING YET?

Small cat in the rocking chair
and a gusting night – spring yet?
The fire has gone out,
wind peers down the chimney
looking for something to eat.
"Don't come in here," I mutter.
Small cat stands, worried;
I fill the stove, send smoke,
give the wind a taste of
cedar, larch, fir,
seasons condensed
like the winter count
of the Lakota.
Fire kindles, crackles, billows,
tree memory rising,
snatched by hungry wind,
carried off under its arm.

LUNCH

I knelt on the dusty ground, facing but not meeting the stare of the African lion poised to rush me. He tensed in a hunting crouch fifteen feet away, eyes dilating. They fixed; he hurtled forward.

I didn't move. The instant before impact he swerved, then turned and whacked me on the jaw with one massive paw.

De-clawed. Even so, my face was numb for some time. My pulse-rate not quite normal either. But this was not an encounter with a free lion; he was captive and would remain so, though not an animal anyone would mistake for tame. De-clawed, he could not be returned to his rightful habitat; neither could he be kept as a "pet". Apparently this dilemma was the case for all the wolves and big cats residing at this fairly remote private facility in NE Washington state.

I was there because Gabriel had done a photo essay on the place for the newspaper. Gabriel had made a favourable impression on the woman who, with her teenage son, cared for these magnificent, wronged animals. One of them, a massive male Siberian wolf who the woman said hated men, cottoned on to Gabriel. So when Gabriel mentioned his hermit mom who got on well with cats, the woman said to bring me over sometime. She didn't usually allow people into the enclosures with the animals, but on assessment decided I might do all right.

I wasn't so sure. I entered the cat enclosure, part of it indoors, part outdoors, that housed a male and female mountain lion (or cougar/puma) and the aforementioned male African lion. (Not long after our visit the cougars were separated from the lion, who had become enamoured of the female cougar.) I'd been warned that the female cougar didn't like women. Sure enough, on entry a superbly athletic cat bounded up, lightly leaping over my shoulders and head, pushing off from me. Roughly. She came at me from everywhere at once, bouncing me off the walls like a squash ball. But she didn't bite.

I rallied, got my back to a wall and stayed still, as relaxed as possible. The one thing you do not want to do around big cats is behave like prey. You don't run, make jerky movements, or allow yourself to be bullied. I held my ground and shoved back when she charged into me. We both calmed down, then. The lithe male, her mate, held aloof. I could relate; clear signals: we would keep some distance, though mutually interested. We checked each other out obliquely, pretending not to.

Meanwhile the African lion, Judah, wanted some fun. Unlike the cougars, Judah came from a socialising lineage of cats. He batted a bowling ball as a housecat does a rubber toy. He liked his tummy rubbed. But was not cute in this; more like a pasha. He had dignity, threat, and power; a carnivore's tummy, and that bigger than most.

I fed him. Raw meat harvested from road-kill deer and ranch-donated cattle. The dripping meat was handed to me over the fence; I offered bloody hunks to Judah. It was scary. I think our hostess was testing my nerve. Other than during the feeding, I found I was more at ease with the cats when I sat or crouched on the ground. Conventional wisdom says to increase safety by making yourself look as tall and imposing as possible, as cats – unlike say, rhinoceri – usually take this

into consideration when deciding on a course of action. Cats don't thrive by being brave but by being canny. Nonetheless I felt safer close to the ground; cat-like, quicker, steadier, stronger, not so anxious.

The male cougar decided to approach. He padded around for a while, first, as though I were invisible. Then veered, coming alongside and brushing me, almost the way a domestic cat rubs your legs. The cougar made an amazingly sweet chirping noise; our hostess said that the cougars only do this when they're intimately conversing with one another. It is such a tiny, happy sound to come from such an intimidating beast. I sat still, didn't try to touch the cougar. He settled not as far away as before.

When Gabriel and I first arrived, we'd gone into the house to feed the African lion cub; the youngest cats lived in the house along with the resident tabbies and dog (who was despised by the lions). The female cougar, though an adult, once stayed on a pallet in the living room during a serious illness. Our hostess got up in the middle of the night to check on the cougar and found her teenage son curled up with the big cat.

Her son was the only one who could effectively deal with Judah – the lion was rapidly approaching his sire's extraordinary 700 pound physique. Judah escaped his enclosure one day, to go after the hated dog. As the boy was wrestling the lion away from the dog, the UPS delivery truck drove up, the driver horrified to see a rampaging lion apparently mauling the youth. The youth, unsavaged, managed to hustle Judah back through the enclosure doorway. Even the dog was unscathed. But the boy's mother confided to me that she had dreams about Judah killing her son.

While I was bottle-feeding the lion cub, and Gabriel was sitting on the sofa chatting with our hostess, a black leopard cub emerged from the kitchen dragging a lump of raw meat. The leopard evidently recalled Gabriel's last visit, as those stunning blue eyes lit up at the sight of my son. Undetected by Gabriel, the cub hurried toward the sofa, dragging the oozing meat, and flung himself and his gory prize over the sofa arm onto Gabriel's lap. Ready to share with his buddy – a vegetarian. But all the same pleased.

We took the cubs outside and they frisked after me into the field. I *wanted* that wee leopard, and knew the folly of that desire. Our hostess described how her domestic cats became apprehensive, then appalled, when cubs – who started out at the bottom of the household feline hierarchy – kept growing bigger and bigger, their play growing rougher and rougher, their paws disproportionate in size and power, until they dwarfed (and terrorised) the tabbies.

This same realisation happens to people who try to domesticate what is wild and should remain so. When I next visited the leopard he was half-grown and no longer comfortable with human proximity. It hurt to see him confined, on exhibit, a poisoned magic. I never went back.

When Judah had completed his feeding he followed to where I sat. We roughhoused more or less congenially, then he phlumped down beside me and began licking the meat juices off my fingers with his huge rasping tongue. Pretty soon my whole hand was in his mouth. Those teeth! Very gently he began gnawing my hand, all the while watching my face. It was the strangest experience – those teeth, those eyes! – my hand gently trapped in the lion's mouth.

His teeth nicked my thumb – I hardly felt it but Judah instantly stopped gnawing and released my hand, never taking his gaze off me. It was understood; in the real world I would've been lunch.

IN THE WORLD OF THE SMALL CAT

In the world of the small cat,

the moon, the sun,

each day's groomed paw,

nothing growing old.

PEAS NOW

Our cat Jumpers had a thing about frozen peas. He had a thing about food, period, but one winter gave me all kinds of grief about peas.

We don't have a refrigerator, much less a freezer, at our place on the mountain. In winter the outdoors is our freezer. Food stays cold in a cooler box outside the door, but Jumpers kept knocking off the weights placed atop the box, pillaging at will. Jumpers has a humongous will.

I took what was left of the frozen peas (a shred of wrapper) and threw it away. I bought more peas. Hung them from the roof eaves, seven feet from the ground. When you don't have much money, and have to hike down a mountain, drive seventy miles roundtrip to the supermarket, then hike up a mountain with your groceries, you become protective of your peas.

That night I was sitting in the armchair, working on a manuscript, when I heard a bad noise outside. A Jumpers noise, one he makes when he is informing something that he is about to kill it.

I investigated; Jumpers was crouched below the package of frozen peas, staring at it like a martial artist, making dire "ack-ack-ack" threats. I prodded him with my foot. "Cut it out." I picked him up and bore him into the house.

Moments later he was back out the catdoor, threatening the peas. I sighed. Then caught my breath – it had gone too quiet out there all the sudden. I sprang up, rushed outside. Horrified to find Jumpers seven feet off the ground, swinging by his teeth from the bag of peas. Not just holding on by his teeth, but ferociously chewing at the same time, through the bag, into the peas.

I had a hell of a tussle prying him loose; when it comes to food Jumpers concedes nothing, not even to me, his best pal. Truly, I get no peas with that cat around.

THE SILENCE OF LIGHT

River winding

through the night

reflecting

stars in our sleep,

a shine

we don't remember.

One night I woke,

hands reaching

for that radiance,

speechless from

long years of passage

it traced

the edges of a pine,

miming a wisdom

that beauty,

like love, is real

even as

the world slumbers.

NIGHT SHIFT

I blew out the candles and went upstairs to bed. A frigid winter night on the mountain, the two cats tunnelled under the blankets; I heard the dog come up the stairs, circle twice and phlump down on the rug, nose tucked into tail.

Light woke me. Living without electricity, you tune to natural cycles of light and dark; you get sleepy when the sun goes down, perky when the sun comes up. You sleep a lot in winter and it doesn't feel like too much; you're wakeful in summer and that feels fine. I couldn't figure out why I was so KNACKERED that winter morning. Like I'd hardly gone to bed.

I groaned, crawled out of bed, dressed, and went downstairs. Piled wood on the fire. Fed the cats. They were avid, impatient as usual. I lit a candle, as it wasn't full light out yet. Sat down with a cup of tea and started working on a manuscript. After some time I paused, puzzled. It wasn't getting any brighter out. Weird. I looked at the clock. 2 am.

I couldn't believe it.

No wonder the cats had been so delighted. I'd only been in bed a couple hours. Moonlight tricked me.

Moonlight on snow must be one of the most magical sights imaginable, especially on the mountain. Snow crystals glitter – jewel colours: sapphire, emerald, ruby, amethyst and, of course, millions of diamonds. That smooth sculpted surface with its jewel gleams; the moon with its perfect roundness, a moonstone so bright the trees cast shadows; ink pools below boulders; the stars are shards of cold light, the Milky Way a shattered porcelain vase. The stillness absolute.

There are full moon nights in winter when Robin and her daughter put on their skis and glide across the field, lie on their backs in the snow and stargaze. Nights when I go outside, restless as a cat, and stand spellbound in the alternate reality of moonlight pouring like milk over an eerie landscape.

Sometimes, when the moon lifts over the cliffs, the coyotes sing.

The night aspect of living close to nature is perhaps the most alien to modern people. This alienation probably started with the use of fire to create domesticity, a separation between humans and other animals. A protection, a security of light and warmth. Amplified, nowadays, to artificially perpetuate our day length and make the sense of vision dominate human perceptual capacities. Sight, more than smell, taste, touch, hearing – and intuition – seems most closely allied with the intellectual part of the brain; just as smell is the most primally-linked sense. In the light we feel most in control, rational, productive. Unease in the dark is basic to most sighted humans unless they are brought up, or have learned, to feel comfortable in that medium.

It took some years, during my early twenties when I started living without electricity, to get past that fear. I realised I was more frightened by the spectre of harm from predatory humans than by any threat from wildlife. Rather than cower in my cabin or stockpile weaponry, there evolved a sense of resource from my surroundings, and an equal valuing of day and night. The more I got to know my habitat, the more solidarity and strength and ease I experienced. The less isolation. In this state of mind light and dark were not adversarial, but complementary.

My husband and I used to go for night walks in Michigan even when there was no moonlight. When you don't use a torch, night vision takes over. Especially peripheral vision. You see in a different way; your brain operates in a different mode. And your other senses become keen; you feel part of the night, almost invisible.

One night we walked down the road with our black cat Taj – who liked walks in the dark, really did become invisible – to a pond full of courting bullfrogs. A balmy night with a feral wisp of breeze. I felt alert but couldn't see a thing – it was that dark. The frogs clammed up at our approach, then one by one took up their frog songs again until the chorus was deafening. Such ardour! We were sound-wrapped in mating fervour: "I love you, baby; won'tcha come to my lily pad." Definitely rousing.

Eventually we stole away, back toward home, leaving the frogs to their procreation rituals. Our movement, however, startled the bejesus out of a bear snacking on berries beside the road. We almost collided with him. The bear's reactive crashing through the berry thicket in turn startled the bejesus out of us.

A tar black night. We couldn't see the bear; the bear couldn't see us. I stood still, figuring I was more likely to blunder into the bear if I tried for evasive action than if I just stayed put. I couldn't tell if the noise now next to me was the bear or my husband. My main worry was the cat; I called his name and felt his body softly bump my legs. I picked him up and waited.

The crashing-through-brambles noises subsided. I heard my husband gently call my name – would've bumped his legs if I could've found them. We continued home – a fine evening's adventure.

On another night my husband and I, and Taj – who still liked these walks – went up a low hill on a different piece of land in Michigan, to sit in the bracken on the slope. This land had once been sand dunes, was still sandy-soiled. A clear creek below the hill threaded past cedars and pines. (I came upon a young porcupine huddled at the top of a young pine there, once – at eye level with me.)

The dense bracken that night was silvered with moonlight. Sitting amidst it with Taj beside us, we listened to the night. Great horned owl. Bats. Mink. Deer. Breeze hushing through the pines. Crickets. The land speaking to itself, a vocabulary of season. The night shift going about its business. The overpowering smell of the bracken, the peace of the cedars. Splash of trout in the creek, plop of frog into the gurgling water. Scurries and squeaks. Taj purring against my leg, flicking his ears. I can't imagine ever feeling this alive and glad sitting in front of a TV.

A city friend from Chicago came to visit on the land in Michigan. He wanted to sleep outside in his tent. Said he felt a spiritual affinity with bears – that Bear was his totem animal. He thought that spending the night in a tent would perhaps bring him into closer communion with Bear.

Halfway through the night I was awakened by a knock on the door. My friend stood clutching his scrumpled sleeping bag to his chest, looking sheepish, harried, disconsolate. "Can I sleep in the house?"

A woeful tale. Just as he was getting to sleep he had been alarmed by rustling outside his tent. It went on and on. He rallied his nerve and peeped out. Porcupines. Worrisome. What if they punctured his tent? Finally they went away. Relieved, he tried to settle himself again. Was just dozing off when – oh no! – major rustling. Branches crackling. Porcupines again? He stuck his head out.

Bear.

This was too much. Totem Bear in his mind was not the same experience as real bear in the night forest, next to his tent. Bugger communing.

Wisdom may be a dance between caution and embrace, experience and understanding. To love what is undomestic has to include acceptance of its reality, a matter of respect as well as affection. Reconciling what is in your head with what is in the forest. When the two become aligned within a clarity of relationship, you might be able to claim, as did Chief Joseph of the Nez Perce, that "The earth and myself are of one mind."

At my father's place in central Oregon, my husband went one night to watch the elk. An Arctic night, no wind, but deathly cold. He followed the elk down to the river, never disturbing them, and after a long time came back half frozen, totally chuffed. The herd had browsed and moved, browsed and moved, in the freezing mist of their own breath. At the river they waded into the shallows as if at a family beach picnic. Young ones gambolled and snorted, teasing each other with nips and splashes. In the grim cold they inhabited a secret warm world of elkness.

To visit, you first make friends with the dark.

WE STAYED

We stayed on the water
long enough to see the
herons finish their day,
hunker on rocks offshore,
necks folded, unspeaking together.
We stayed,
waves lifting and
lowering the dinghy,
to see the rose and gold and
heron-blue light
cupped in ripples,
seals glistening and sliding in
and out of
that flickering
in the blue shadow
of Knoydart's hills.
Evening wind in the
darkening season, the space
between island
and mainland, the fullness
bereft between my son's visit
and leave-taking;
a coolness – my shudder as we
drifted toward Mallaig,
losing grasp of the day, a place
farther than great-grandparents or
crossings Hebridean.
We stayed until the tide went out,
the colours draining westward.